C000003232

Where Two Rivers Meet

Russian Windows on the Gospel

— NICOLA VIDAMOUR —

FOREWORD BY
PÁDRAIG Ó TUAMA

Sacristy
Press

Sacristy Press
PO Box 612, Durham, DH1 9HT

www.sacristy.co.uk

First published in 2022 by Sacristy Press, Durham

Copyright © Nicola Vidamour 2022
The moral rights of the author have been asserted.

All rights reserved, no part of this publication may be reproduced or transmitted in any form or by any means, electronic, mechanical photocopying, documentary, film or in any other format without prior written permission of the publisher.

Bible extracts, unless otherwise stated, are from the *New Revised Standard Version Bible: Anglicized Edition*, copyright 1989, 1995, Division of Christian Education of the National Council of the Churches of Christ in the United States of America. Used by permission. All rights reserved.

Icons copyright © Псково-Изборский объединенный музей-заповедник, г. Псков, Россия, 2022.

Every reasonable effort has been made to trace the copyright holders of material reproduced in this book, but if any have been inadvertently overlooked the publisher would be glad to hear from them.

Sacristy Limited, registered in England
& Wales, number 7565667

British Library Cataloguing-in-Publication Data
A catalogue record for the book is available
from the British Library

ISBN 978–1–78959–228–3

For my mum, Mollie Priest
Looby loo
Her way of saying the Russian for "I love you"

Vechnaya Pamyat (Eternal Memory)

Paul Nicholas Priest (1944–2000)
who gave me life, faith and a love for travel

John Christopher Dewey (1942–2019)
who gave me Russian

Contents

Foreword v
Acknowledgements. viii

Chapter 1. In the beginning 1
Chapter 2. Where two rivers meet 11
Chapter 3. Put the kettle on 23
Chapter 4. Mary gets evangelized. 33

Little Window 1. 42

Chapter 5. A parent's sacrifice 45
Chapter 6. The Passion of Pushkin. 55

Little Window 2. 63

Chapter 7. Entering the city 67
Chapter 8. Clean Thursday. 77
Chapter 9. The Women Myrrh-Bearers. 87
Chapter 10. To hell and back 97
Chapter 11. Lost in translation 107
Chapter 12. Homecoming. 117

Postscript 124

Foreword

There's an old phrase in Irish—*bíonn siúlach scéalach*—translating to something like "travellers have tales to tell", or, more directly: "those who walk have stories". I kept on thinking of this phrase while reading Nicola Vidamour's book: the contours of language, art, theology, travel, curiosity, self-doubt and intellect all shine through.

I first met Nicola when I was invited to speak on a retreat. It was a weeklong retreat, and every evening, Nicola would lead a reflection meeting with the team. Not normally a fan of meetings, I found myself looking forward to those meetings: Nicola would go from detail, to reflection, to a joke, to a sexual innuendo, to a linguistic quip from one sentence to another. I came away from that retreat with a new group of friends, Nicola one of them. I was determined to keep in touch.

From the opening sentence of this book, you see her intelligence, playfulness and respect for language. "In the beginning was the word and the word was *Zdravstvuyte*". Who writes like this? Even before the translation, I know I'm in the company of someone whose love for both theology and language is seamless. Time and time again, Nicola folds us into the place in her—her heart,

I'm sure—where prayer and communication originate. Here, Russian mixes with iconography, loneliness mixes with connection, theology mixes with history, war mixes with doubt.

As I write, I'm checking the news for what's happening today in Ukraine. And Russia is, once again, a byword for danger. *Where Two Rivers Meet* is timely. Nicola Vidamour speaks from the hearth of language, a place where the deepest impulses of peace might reside. And she also speaks from the hearth of persecution: people of faith had, for decades, been persecuted in the former USSR. And then, as some freedoms were experienced, internal tensions towards smaller religious minorities—Methodism being one of them—were codified and communicated.

It's said that when the Israelites crossed the Red Sea, and then began singing their song of victory and praise as they escaped the Egyptian persecutors that God silenced the angels from singing because children of his hand were drowning. The biblical witness is clear about war: side with the persecuted, work for their safety, seek peace. But the biblical witness is also clear that enmity will, finally, reap its own rotten fruits. Nicola's exploration of these strands of Russian faith, community, connection, hospitality and creativity is a testament to that which is betrayed by the actions of war-making leaders.

Where Two Rivers Meet explores language, and hospitality, and the story of a life. It also explores a change in the imagination of mission. Where before a person went as a stranger into a land, seeking converts, we hear, in Nicola's story, the story of a person going with open hands seeking friends, seeking exchange, seeking to be converted, and seeking to deepen love. An icon is a window into God. This book is a window into what it means to be a person of faith seeking to learn a new language: across cultures, across Christianities, across barriers, across the chasms created in the wake of wars, accusations and aggressions.

What are these two rivers? They—like every river— keep changing: one is England, one is Russia; one is one language, the other is another; one is faith, the other is exploration; one is liturgy, the other is change; one is male, the other is female; one is tradition, the other is innovation; one is beginnings, the other is endings; one is protest, the other is prayer. In Nicola Vidamour's *Where Two Rivers Meet*, we are invited to a conversation that has sustained her, and in this invitation, we are asked to consider which rivers meet in us, and how, and what language they speak, and what they're saying.

Pádraig Ó Tuama

Acknowledgements

The Russian word for thank you—*spasibo*—literally means "God save you". I would like to say *spasibo* to the following people:

- My mum—for her courage in letting me go and her boundless joy at every place of meeting.
- My sister, Rachel, and my nephews, James and Benjamin, who always make me feel rooted and loved.
- My pre-Pskov soul friends who have kept in touch across the years and across the miles: Georgia Birri, Margaret Crinyion, Chad Gandiya, Bronwen Gray, Russell Ogston, Tania Ortu, Debbie and Martin Priddey, Magdalen Smith and Sally Stutz.
- My friends in Russia—especially Konstantin Ababkov, Galina Galaktionova, Eduard Khegay, Nelli Mamonova, Yulia Parygina and Rimma Plyashchenko.
- My Russian Orthodox friends in France—Anne and Paul Janin, Kira Korelsky and Paul, Bishop of Tracheia.
- Hans Växby—for helping me to see God's grace in every snowflake.

- Wilma Dewey—the mirror of John's poetic soul.
- Steve Pearce and the Asia-Pacific Methodist Mission Partners, who explored some of this material with me in Thailand in July 2017.
- My Methodist sisters who reflected on several of these icons with me at the Women Ministers' Annual Gathering on Zoom in November 2020.
- Friends and colleagues who helped to source and provide some of the material used in this book: Ellen Farmer, Andriana Vasiliadis, Kim Weston, Bob and Patty Williams, and Andrew Maguire.
- The Methodist Church in Britain—with particular gratitude for the gift of a sabbatical, the Global Relationships Team, and the districts and circuits in which I have served.
- The Woughton Ecumenical Partnership and the Milton Keynes Methodist Circuit—with special thanks to Ian Herbert, Iola Samuels and Nicola Martyn-Beck.
- The Community for Spiritual Formation—especially Sheryl Anderson, Jill Baker, James Bamber, Kenneth Boyd-Browne and Andrew Lightowler—who always help me reconnect with what is life-giving.
- The Pskov Museum (Псково-Изборский объединенный музей-заповедник) for being so flexible and helpful with the legal agreement to reproduce the icons at a time when British-Russian relationships were at an all-time low.

- The Nicholas Roerich Museum in New York for their generous provision of the image for the front cover.
- The team at Sacristy Press for their encouragement, support and gentle guidance.
- Pádraig Ó Tuama, whose passion for words and the Word moves and inspires me.
- Pyotr Ilyich Tchaikovsky—for music which articulates what words cannot express.

My Letters from Pskov were first published in the *Methodist Recorder*.

In the beginning

In the beginning was the word, and the word was *Zdravstvuyte*.

I sat in the back row feeling very uncooperative. In fact, I would have described myself as *bolshie*—having no idea at the time that this was a Russian word. (*Bolshie* is a shortened version of Bolshevik which comes from the Russian word *bolshoi*, meaning big. In British slang, it means "defiant and rebellious".) It was a sunny day, and I had been very reluctant to come inside and attend the lunch-hour meeting with Mr Dewey. Mr Dewey taught German and Russian at Bournemouth School for Girls. He did not have enough people to make the Russian class viable, so he had called a meeting of all those who had chosen to do German to try and persuade us to do Russian instead. I had no intention of changing my mind. There were about forty girls in the room, and, for some reason, Mr Dewey picked on me.

"This is the Russian word for Hello," he said. "*Zdravstvuyte*. Can you say it?"

"No!" came my bolshie response.

"Go on. Give it a try," said Mr Dewey.

So, I did. "*Zdravstvuyte*".

"That was very good," said Mr Dewey. "You should learn Russian."

So, I did.

This decision was to have a major impact on the rest of my life—although I did not know it then. It was 1985, and Mikhail Gorbachev had just become General Secretary of the Communist Party of the Soviet Union. *Glasnost* (openness) and *perestroika* (restructuring)—the words used to describe the reforms which Gorbachev initiated—were early additions to my Russian vocabulary. Other early words were жук (*zhuk*) meaning beetle because the beetle-like design of the first letter helped me and the other girls in Mr Dewey's class to learn the new alphabet. The Russian word for woman (*zhenshchina*) also begins with the same letter, and I have used that since to help foreign visitors in Russia work out which is the female toilet. You might find beetles in there!

I soon fell in love with Russian. I enjoyed languages, but I was getting a bit bored with French. Russian was so different. The alphabet, literature and culture took me into a whole new world and fed the hunger which I was beginning to recognize in myself for the other.

The Other, with a capital "O", is also a way of describing God, and my decision to start learning Russian coincided with the first stage of my sense of call to ordained ministry. These two significant developments in my life felt completely unconnected, but they happened in the same year. This was the point at which two rivers found their source and began to flow towards one another.

The church I attended during my teenage years had a strong tradition of putting on Christian musicals. In 1984, we performed *Greater than Gold*, which told the story of Mary Jones, a Welsh girl who was desperate to have a Bible in her own language. She saved up for six years, and in 1800, at the age of fifteen, set off to walk the twenty-eight miles to Bala, where she expected to be able to buy a Welsh Bible. Her story led to the founding of the Bible Society, which is still providing Bibles for people today in their mother tongue. I was chosen to play the part of Mary, and I felt a deep connection with her. I realized how important the Bible was to me too. I wanted to help ensure that people everywhere were able to access this precious gift in their own language.

In the meantime, Mr Dewey was unlocking the treasure-trove of Russian literature for me. He introduced me to Pushkin and Chekhov, Zamyatin and Akhmatova. I was converted and was soon convinced that God was a Russian speaker, and that Russian must surely be the language of heaven.

This conviction was strengthened by my first experience of Russian Orthodox worship. One Sunday, I boarded a National Express coach from Bournemouth to London. I was going to a concert at the Royal Albert Hall in the afternoon and had decided to go up earlier in the day and attend the morning service at one of the Methodist churches in central London. Anne, the French language *assistante* from school, happened to be on the same coach. By now, I was doing my A levels (Russian, French and Religious Studies). At 9 a.m. on Monday mornings, I had a French conversation class with Anne. At our first class, she asked what other subjects I was studying. When I mentioned Russian, she got very excited. Her grandparents (both maternal and paternal) were all Russians who had emigrated to France in the early 1920s, and she had been brought up bilingually. "Come at 8:30 a.m. on Mondays," she said, "and we can have a Russian conversation class before the French one." So I did.

Anne told me that she was travelling to London so that she could attend worship at the Russian Orthodox Cathedral in Ennismore Gardens—not far from the Royal Albert Hall. She invited me to go with her and I accepted. I was transported to another place by the beauty and mystery of the worship. I completely understood why the envoys whom Prince Vladimir of Kyiv sent to experience worship at the Hagia Sophia in Constantinople came back and said that they did not know whether they were in heaven or earth.

When Anne completed her year in Bournemouth, she kindly invited me to spend the Easter holidays with her in Paris. This gave me intense practice in both languages. Anne's mother, who was also a teacher, would turn the kitchen radio on and then ask me questions in Russian about what was being broadcast in French!

I was also given full immersion into Orthodox Holy Week, attending most of the services (and even singing in the choir) at the church of Sainte-Geneviève-des-Bois.

This worship—especially the Easter liturgy, when we processed three times around the cemetery at midnight, came back to find the dark church ablaze with light, and joyfully and repeatedly proclaimed "*Christos voskres*" (Christ is risen)—moved me deeply. I could feel two rivers—Methodism and Orthodoxy—surging within me, and I did not know which one to follow.

The priest at Sainte-Geneviève-des-Bois was an Englishman called Father Paul. One evening, I was invited to dinner at his home, and during the meal, he asked lots of questions about the Methodist Church. When I gave an affirmative answer to his question about whether women could be ordained in the Methodist Church, he then looked at me with his piercing blue eyes and said: "And do you have such a vocation?" I looked back at him and said: "That's something I am struggling with at the moment." "I know you are, Nicola," he said. "I know you are."

That conversation affected me profoundly. It confirmed for me that my vocation was in Methodism and not in Orthodoxy. It was also significant because Father Paul was the first person who recognized my vocation without knowing my father. My father was a Methodist minister, and when people suggested that I might follow in his footsteps, I had been dismissive, assuming that this was only because we had a similar character and temperament. Now that someone who had never met my father had seen something in me, I had to pay attention.

When it came to deciding what to study at university, I was not sure whether to choose Russian or theology. It was clear to me that one day, I could well end up studying theology as part of my training for ordination. So I opted to study Russian, which was really my favourite subject anyway. I got a place on a four-year course at Bristol University which included the possibility of spending the whole of the third year in Russia. I also started training to become a Methodist local (lay) preacher—a requirement for offering for ordination.

In my first term at Bristol, I saw a flyer in the Chaplaincy Centre, advertising a three-day conference at Salisbury and Wells Theological College for students wanting to explore a sense of vocation. I signed up immediately. The conference took place in early January, soon after the feast of the Epiphany, and so the story of the Magi in the second chapter of Matthew's Gospel was an important focus. We were asked to share which word or phrase in the story particularly stood out for us. I was struck by the fact that the star had appeared in the east which, for me, symbolized Eastern Europe. I was still grappling with how to combine my love of Russian with my growing sense of call to ordained ministry.

My third year, abroad, felt like an opportunity to "do a Jonah", as I thought of it at the time, and run away from God or, at least, from Methodism. Jonah was a prophet whom God wanted to send to Nineveh. Jonah did not want to go there and got on a boat going somewhere else. My whole life had been spent in the Methodist Church, and I felt that going to a place where there were no Methodists would help me to test my call.

I joined a ten-month programme in Moscow which was organized by the RLUSC (Russian Language Undergraduate Study Committee). I was one of twenty-three students selected from different universities across Britain. We had twelve hours of classes each week at the Moscow Linguistic University which left plenty of time for other activities. Most of us took the opportunity to get some relevant experience for the career paths we envisaged for ourselves. I decided to volunteer in a soup kitchen.

My journal for that year mentions food nearly every day. I can still remember my excitement and delight on the day when I found cauliflowers being sold on the street! However, there was absolutely no danger of us being as desperate for food as the pensioners who attended the soup kitchen. We had the luxury of being able to buy supplies from the British Embassy shop and from other well-stocked stores which only accepted foreign currency. I also received regular food parcels from my church at home. The experience of that year taught me that some rivers can never meet. Wealth and poverty, for example, may flow alongside one another, but there is always a steep bank which separates them.

The two rivers flowing within me had to diverge from one another the following summer when I was awarded my Russian degree and accredited as a Methodist local preacher. It was a wrench to give up the Russian I loved, but the call to offer for ordained ministry had an even stronger pull on me. I did try to use my Russian during the year it took to go through the candidating (selection) process and even had an interview at GCHQ (Government Communications Headquarters)—an intelligence agency of the British Government. I ended up working in a bookshop at Piccadilly Circus.

Eight years later, when I was in the penultimate year of my first appointment as a Methodist minister, I went to see my District Chair (the senior minister with pastoral oversight of me) to discuss where I might serve next. During my theological training, I had spent three months at TTS (Tamilnadu Theological Seminary) in South India which had rekindled my yearning for "the other". I had consequently asked to be given a multicultural inner-city appointment when I left college but had been sent to a village in Surrey. I told my District Chair that I had a niggle about serving overseas and so would like to repeat my request for a multicultural appointment as a way of testing this call. Was it enough for me to be in a context where the world was around me? Or did I need to go and live in another country myself?

My District Chair asked me why I was not offering to go overseas immediately. I told him that I felt I would not get through the selection process, because it would look as though I was trying to run away from pain and loss. In the preceding two years, I had been through a divorce and my father had died. My District Chair encouraged me to offer for overseas service and see what happened. So I did.

I had no strong preference for which part of the world I would like to go to, and so I made a completely open offer. I was vaguely aware that there was now a Methodist presence in Russia, but I did not even consider that going there might be a possibility. The outcome of the process was that the World Church team decided that they were going to send me to Argentina. "If you can learn Russian," they said, "Spanish will be a doddle!" The Methodist Church plans who will go where so far in advance that it was still a couple of years before I was due to get on a plane. A few months later, there was a financial crisis in Argentina and the church there decided that this was not a good time to be receiving someone from overseas. So somewhere else had to be found for me.

About this time, the World Methodist Conference was taking place in Brighton, and I went to serve as an interpreter for one of the Russian participants. Through talking to her, I realized that the Methodist Church in Russia was much bigger than I had realized and that there might well be a role for me there. I therefore asked the World Church team if we could knock on Russia's door. I was still open to other options as well, but it seemed sensible to make use of the Russian language and cultural awareness which I already had.

I was thrilled and excited when, after many months of anxious waiting, I got the news that I was being invited to become the pastor of a Methodist congregation in St Petersburg. The two rivers flowing inside me were finally able to meet. I could combine my love for Russian with my love for Methodism!

2

Where two rivers meet

April 2003

"Moscow! Moscow! Moscow!" Four little children come running up to the departure gate as fast as their snow boots can carry them, shouting out their destination with joy, excitement and impatience. Their simple cry articulates much of what I am feeling as I wait to board my plane at Heathrow. A few hours later, Moscow lies before us: little wooden dachas, surrounded by snow; Ikea and McDonalds on the way in from the airport; rows and rows of identical-looking high-rise apartment blocks— one of which, on Lenin Avenue, becomes my home.

Within ten days, I am immersed in the rhythm of my new life. At 7:45 a.m., I leave the apartment, lock the steel door four times, walk down eight flights of stairs, catch the trolleybus to the metro station and then the metro to the Methodist Seminary. I attend the Exegesis class taught by Valentina Kusnetsova, who has published a wonderful modern translation of the New Testament. She draws some inspiring and thought-provoking parallels between the Gospel stories and life in Russia. She talks about the story of the Widow's Mite in connection with the vast amounts of money spent rebuilding the Cathedral of Christ the Saviour; and Judas' betrayal in relation to the way in which people betrayed their family and friends during the Stalinist purges.

After lunch at the seminary—the students take it in turns to provide this each day—I take the metro to my three-hour one-to-one language class at the Inlingua Centre on Tverskaya, one of the main streets in central Moscow. My teacher, Natalya, is rather bemused when she asks for my views on ecumenism, and I think she has asked me about communism! We plough through endless grammar drills as well as discussing religious literature and contemporary fiction. I practise reading aloud the Eucharistic Prayer and other liturgical texts.

At 5 p.m., I walk through Red Square as the church bells are ringing and cross the river—which was completely frozen when I arrived but is now beginning to flow freely—to the Alexander Men Orthodox Seminary. Here I attend lectures on the Hebrew Bible, Orthodox Liturgy, Christianity and Art, Russian Religious Thought. The classroom window looks out on St Basil's Cathedral—beautifully illuminated at night—and, with a bearded priest teaching theology in my favourite language, I am in heaven.

By 10 p.m., I am home again, hopefully with enough energy to do the homework for my language class. The language class even happens on Saturday morning—but then I am free to do my shopping and laundry and to go to the theatre. So far, I have been to see two operas at the Bolshoi Theatre—Eugene Onegin *and* The Queen of Spades. *And* Nord-Est—*the brilliant Russian musical which was the scene of a hostage crisis in 2002 when Chechen terrorists stormed the theatre during the show.*

On my first visit to the Bolshoi, I got soundly rebuked by a woman in the queue for the toilet. She told me that I should tuck my cross inside my clothing, because it is a symbol of faith not a decoration. I have since been told the same by another babushka *(the Russian word for a grandmother or a woman old enough to have grandchildren), so I am now dutifully wearing it next to my skin. It is such a contrast to the exchange I had with a* babushka *twelve years ago who was so excited to see me wearing my cross openly because she had had to hide hers away all her life.*

I have been to a number of different worship services. The first weekend I went to the American Protestant Chaplaincy with Tom and Nancy Hoffmann—a Methodist couple from the States who are working as Church Development Officers here. The congregation is mainly black, and I was disturbed to hear about the violent racist attacks many of them had suffered on the metro. This congregation still runs the soup kitchen where I used to work twelve years ago. I have visited the Korean Methodist Congregation in Moscow twice and really felt at home there. It was fascinating to hear people tell their stories about when their family moved to Russia. Some stories went back to Catherine the Great. I felt far less comfortable when I went with Igor, one of the students at the Methodist Seminary, to his church. There was a woman pastor, and yet all the women had their heads covered; songs about the wrath of God were sung to jolly Russian folk tunes, and the service lasted for three hours. What I was impressed by—as I have been in all the churches I have visited—is the significant lay involvement in the services. At Igor's church, everyone in the twelve-strong congregation led some part of the worship.

Three weeks after moving into my apartment, I had to move into a new one because a visiting American professor was coming to teach at the seminary and needed to live there. Two weeks after moving into my new apartment, I was on the overnight train from Moscow to Tallinn (Estonia). My visa was due to expire the following day, and I needed to leave the country to obtain a new one. I will remember the train journey for the energetic Russian customs official who burst into our compartment at 5 a.m. and took great pleasure in searching everyone's luggage and throwing the contents back at them. He was really interested in my Russian Bible—a gift from the Bible Society before I left home—and stunned to discover that I could read it without translation.

On arrival in Tallinn, I was met by my roommate, Rosita, a thirty-year-old from Lithuania. We hit it off very quickly. She is an only child and delights in calling me her little sister. That is a true reflection of how deep and special our relationship is. The Baltic Methodist Theological Seminary is an amazing facility—purpose-built with

Korean money three years ago. The lectures are in Estonian, but simultaneous Russian translation is provided on headphones. I am going to preach my first sermon in Russian at the seminary service this coming Wednesday. On Saturday, I went with the youth workers from the Russian-speaking congregation to a young offenders' institution in another town. It was difficult to understand the boys because they were all talking at once and using a lot of slang and what I can only presume were Russian swear words. However, I did my best to answer their questions about life in England. What slang names do we have for policemen? Had I ever met David Beckham? Why do we have a Queen and not a President?

I might have had a more ready answer if they had asked me why British Methodism does not have bishops. The Methodist Church in Russia is part of the United Methodist Church and has a different structure of governance from the British Methodist Church. I cannot put into words how I felt when the bishop told me at the beginning of March that I would not be going to St Petersburg after all because he had found someone else to serve the congregation there. I had a very tearful couple of days as I struggled to make sense of yet another loss in my life. I am deeply grateful for the emails, phone calls, cards, letters, prayers and chocolate parcels which have come my way in response to this news. I am now dreaming new dreams about living and working in Pskov. I plan to go and spend a weekend there once I get back to Russia next month.

The Methodist Church in Britain had never sent anyone to serve in Russia before. So after one term of mission training at the United College of the Ascension in Selly Oak, Birmingham, I was sent to Moscow for my second term of training. It was ten years since I had used my Russian, and church language has a whole vocabulary of its own. So I attended Methodist and Orthodox lectures to listen and learn how Russians talk about God. I also had some private language tuition to help me lead worship clearly and confidently.

I was devastated when I was called into the bishop's office a few weeks after arriving and told that the invitation to serve in St Petersburg had been withdrawn. I was given the choice of going to Yekaterinburg or Pskov instead. Though my tears, I asked Bishop Rüdiger Minor what the nature of the work would be in these two places. He explained that the focus in Yekaterinburg would be mainly youth work and that Pskov were looking for someone to help in all aspects of church life. For this reason, together with the fact that Pskov was much closer to home (and to St Petersburg), I chose Pskov.

Pskov is situated on the western border of Russia, close to the Baltic states of Estonia, Latvia and Lithuania. The overnight train journey from Moscow takes twelve hours. My first memory of the city is being met at the railway station at 8 a.m. by Nelli Mamonova and her husband Valeri. Nelli was the pastor of Pskov United Methodist Church and also served as the District

Superintendent. This meant that she had oversight of four other churches—two in Kaliningrad, one in Belarus and one in Smolensk. Travelling to these churches involved long and complicated journeys, and so she had asked the bishop if he could send someone to help keep the day-to-day life of the Pskov church going whilst she was away. The congregation in Pskov had also acquired a house with some land which they planned to convert into a church building. Overseeing this project was going to take a lot of Nelli's time and energy too.

As we drove up October Street, which runs from the railway station to Lenin Square, I was confronted by "the other", but this time I felt more fear than excitement. I looked out of the car window, desperately searching for something familiar, but none of the shops and cafes I had grown used to in Moscow seemed to have branches here. It felt like a barren land, and my heart began to sink. When we reached Lenin Square, dominated by a Soviet statue of the man himself on a pedestal, we turned left onto Riga Avenue and crossed the river. At this point, a trickle of hope began to flow. Towering above the riverbank was the sturdy white cathedral of the Holy Trinity. The golden domes, glistening in the grey sky, lifted my spirits.

I was later to discover the legend about this site. Olga, the grandmother of Prince Vladimir of Kyiv (who sent the envoys to Constantinople in 987), was born in Pskov. One day, when she was standing on the riverbank, she had a vision of three rays of light coming down from heaven and converging at the point where two rivers meet. She took that as a sign that there would be a great city in this place and commissioned the building of a Cathedral to the Holy Trinity.

The river we crossed in the car is called the Velikaya (Great) River, and it merges with the Pskov River in the centre of town. Whenever I felt homesick, this point—where two rivers meet—was one of two places I would go. These two rivers helped me to reflect on the many double strands I was experiencing within myself. These included English and Russian (as languages); British and Russian (as nationalities and cultures); Methodism and Russian Orthodoxy; the Methodist Church in Britain and the United Methodist Church; home and abroad; heaven and earth; intimacy and solitude; darkness and light; winter and spring; cold and warmth; self and other; poetry and prose; beauty and pain; contemplation and action; body and soul; the head and the heart.

The other place I would go (especially when it was too cold to be outside for long) was the icon rooms in the Pskov Museum. Pskov had a famous icon school, and the museum collection contains many icons which were formerly housed in local churches. There was a reverent and hushed atmosphere in this part of the museum. I very rarely met anyone else there—other than the *babushki* (plural of *babushka*) who were positioned in every room. Some were having a quiet snooze. Others were quick to criticize me for my posture or my lack of interest in their favourite exhibit.

I would always go and visit my favourite set of icons— the festival row from the church of the Archangels Michael and Gabriel in Pskov. This church was built from 1339–40, and the icons date from the first half of the sixteenth century. They came to the Pskov Museum in 1925, were seized by the Germans during the Second World War and returned to the museum after 1945.

Russian Orthodox Churches have an iconostasis—a screen of icons with central and side doors—which separates the altar area from the main body of the church. The iconostasis normally has five rows. The fifth (top) row is for the patriarchs of the Old Testament from Adam to Moses. The fourth row is for the prophets. The third row is the festival row which includes icons of the major festival days of the church year. The second row is the Deesis row which has an icon of Christ on his heavenly throne in the centre and icons of saints on either side. The first (bottom) row is the local row for icons of saints who are particularly significant for this church, including the saint(s) whose name the church has been given.

The icons in this festival row in the museum became my friends. I would look at them, and they would look at me. Sometimes we would have important things to say to one another. On other days, we would simply enjoy being together in companionable silence. These icons helped to root me where I was, whatever season of the church year I was living through emotionally and spiritually at that time. This did not necessarily correspond to the actual season. They also enabled me to journey to a different place—or at least glimpse it through a window.

Icons are often described as windows and the Russian word for icon—икона (*ikona*) is not dissimilar to the Russian word for window—окно (*okno*). Icons are windows into heaven. Sometimes the iconostasis can seem like a barrier—particularly for women who are never allowed to go behind it! Seeing it as a window instead—through which we now only see dimly but will one day see face to face (1 Corinthians 13:12)—helped me to overcome the frustration I often felt at not being able to see what was happening behind the screen.

I mentioned earlier that the iconostasis also has doors. When I first started attending Orthodox worship and was not used to standing for long periods, I was always quite relieved when the doors closed because that meant it was permissible to sit down for a while. The doors open when something significant is about to happen and Christ is drawing closer to the people.

The royal doors are in the centre, and these are used only by the bishop or priest when he is carrying the Gospel book or the chalice containing the Eucharist. In other words, these doors are the gateway though which Christ is revealed to the people. This is emphasized by the tradition of leaving these doors open all the time for seven days after Easter to symbolize the open door of the tomb.

The two side doors are used by the deacons. One of the friends who came to visit me whilst I was living in Russia and attended a Russian Orthodox service with me said she felt the deacons were giving the heavenly notices. "They keep popping out," she said, "to tell us what's going on in heaven!"

I grew up in the era of the British children's television programme *Play School.* Each episode included a film of the world outside the studio which would be shown through one of three different-shaped windows on the set. Viewers would be asked to guess which window would be used today and were then invited to look though that particular window. I am going to invite you now to look with me through the different "windows" of that festival row in the Pskov Museum. I hope this window-gazing will give you a glimpse into the life of people in Russia; into my life and your own inner life; and into the life of Christ. Perhaps you will also discover, as I did, that these are all places where two rivers meet.

3

Put the kettle on

Lent 2005

"Ostorozhno. Dveri zakryvayutsya," *says the announcer on the Moscow and St Petersburg metro every time a train is ready to leave the station. "Be careful. The doors are closing." At a time in the church year when we journey with Jesus' disciples from their hiding place behind closed doors to the tomb with a miraculously open door, I want to share with you some tales from a Russian threshold.*

The main door of the apartment block where I live is fitted with a code. You have to press three numbers simultaneously in order to get into the building. Recently this lock got jammed. It could be opened from the inside but not from the outside. Consequently, there was one occasion when I had to stand on the threshold—in freezing temperatures—until someone happened to come out of the building and let me in. Later that day the lock was completely removed, and we had a residents' meeting to discuss the installation of a domaphone. Dom *is the Russian word for house, and so a* domaphone *is a system where every apartment is equipped with a telephone linked to the main door. Visitors buzz your apartment, and you can then decide whether or not to let them in.*

Once inside the building there are still a number of doors to get through. This is a nine-storey "house", so most people use the lift—at least on the way up. The lift doors close after seven seconds which just about gives time for two people to get in or out, but if there is a third or fourth person, they will probably get left behind. Once you have reached the required floor, there are four apartments to choose from—two to the left and two to the right. Most of these pairings have a joint door into a little corridor— where snowy boots can be left—and then there are separate doors into each of the apartments.

Russians never come and visit without bringing something "for the table". If someone invites you to pop round for a cup of tea, it is expected that you will bring a packet of tea with you—if not a cake or a jar of jam! These gifts, however, must not be handed over until you have walked through the door. It is considered to be a very bad omen if you make your presentation across the threshold.

Russian doors can be very intimidating—whichever side of them you find yourself on—and I have been instructed countless times not to answer my doorbell unless I am expecting someone. Having spent most of my life in Methodist manses where there has always been an open-door policy, it feels very strange living a more enclosed way of life here in Russia. Nevertheless, it remains a great joy to be part of a culture which is no longer trying to lock the gospel behind closed doors but is prepared to cross the threshold from the cross to the empty tomb and receive the gift of eternal life.

"Listen! I am standing at the door, knocking; if you hear my voice and open the door, I will come in to you and eat with you and you with me" (Revelation 3:20).

I was brought up to seat guests comfortably in the lounge and then bring through a pot of tea or coffee on a tray, ideally with some homemade cake arranged on a doily-covered plate. It was a bit of a shock in Russia to find that guests would walk straight into the kitchen. I had learnt at school that that the Russian word for lounge was *gostinnaya*—from the word *gost*, meaning guest. I discovered that what I would describe as the lounge was actually known as the *bolshaya komnata* (big room). This was often a sleeping space as well with the sofa doubling as a bed. Food and drink would only be taken in there for celebrations like birthdays and New Year, when there were more people (and dishes) than the small kitchen table could accommodate. The icon of the Old Testament Trinity—also known as the "Hospitality of Abraham"—reminds me of the scene in a typical Russian kitchen. The guests are perched on hard stools or benches without any back support, and the hosts hover behind them, refilling cups and making sure they have everything they need.

I once showed Andrei Rublev's version of this icon to a Women's Fellowship group in Britain and asked them what they thought it was. "That looks like a group of people having a cup of tea and a good chat," said one of them. In British church life, we often use the word "fellowship" to describe the socializing that takes place after a service, often accompanied by refreshments. One way of translating fellowship into Russian is to use the word *obshcheniye*, which comes from a root meaning "common". It is this word which is used in the Russian Bible to describe the fellowship (or communion) of the Holy Spirit (2 Corinthians 13:13). However, the word normally used to describe the fellowship after a service at church is *chaepitiye*, which literally means "tea-drinking".

After I had recovered from the shock of seeing my guests taking a seat in the kitchen, I was then even more surprised when they reached into their bags and put some biscuits, pastries, cake or chocolate on the table. "This is *k chayu*"—towards the tea—they would say. I learnt very quickly that hospitality in Russia is not about being the hostess with the mostest. It is about everyone bringing something to the table. This is the case not only with friends in your own home but with strangers on long overnight train journeys. Anything put on the table is for everyone to share. What's more, in every train carriage there is a huge urn of hot water from which passengers can go and help themselves at any time of day or night. Mugs and tea bags, bread and sausage meat, cabbage pie and boiled eggs are put on the common table—and the fellowship begins.

The shock and surprise evoked in me by the behaviour of my Russian guests and travel companions is echoed by the experience of Abraham and Sarah in the story depicted by the icon of the Old Testament Trinity (Genesis 18:1–15). Abraham sees three men approaching his tent in the heat of the day and immediately offers them hospitality—water to wash their feet, rest under the tree and some refreshments. He is clearly not expecting that these guests also have something to offer him. Sarah laughs when these men announce that she is going to have a son: she and Abraham are too old for this to be possible. This is a kind of culture shock—akin to what I sometimes felt in Russia—when our long-held expectations and assumptions are suddenly challenged and questioned. This is where two rivers meet—the river of laughter which can flow into or out of a river of tears; the river which has dried up in a barren land; and the river which is bursting its banks like a pregnant woman about to give birth; the rivers which meet when we dare to open the flap of our tent wide enough so that we can see more than passing feet and are moved out of our comfort zone into a deeper encounter.

This icon is known as the Old Testament Trinity because the three angels are seen as the three persons of the Trinity. When you read Genesis 18, these three angels are described as "the Lord" as if they are one person. Most of the time, they appear to speak in unison. Traditional interpretations of the icon suggest that the Son is in the centre, looking towards the Father, whilst the Spirit (who looks pregnant to me!) sits in front of Sarah. It is quite unusual to have the Trinity included as part of the festival row of an iconostasis—except in Pskov where this is quite common. This may be due to the role of the Trinity (the three rays of light seen by Princess Olga) in the legend of the founding of the city.

In the Western church, Trinity Sunday is celebrated a week after Pentecost Sunday. In the Russian Orthodox church year, the feast of the Trinity is on the same day as the feast of Pentecost, as both feasts are a celebration of the coming of the Holy Spirit. The feast of the Trinity is also known in Russia as Green Sunday. The priests wear green vestments, as the Spirit does in this icon, and people bring greenery into their churches and homes. This is a sign of the new life which the Spirit brings and may also be connected with the Jewish harvest festival—known in Greek as Pentecost—which is why there was such an international gathering in Jerusalem when the Spirit came (Acts 2:1–11).

The feet of the two angels at the front of the icon are positioned so that one foot is pointing towards us as we look at them, and the other foot is pointing to the empty space between them. These feet seem to be inviting us to take our place at the table. The Holy Trinity wants to offer hospitality to us. That is what icons do —especially this one. They draw us in. They invite us to enter into this fellowship and to share in this communion.

In the previous chapter, I described icons as windows. I sometimes suggest to people who are engaging with an icon for the first time that they might like to imagine that they are looking at this scene through a window. What do you notice? What draws your attention? What is going on?

With this particular icon, I like to imagine myself on the threshold, just as Abraham was sitting at the entrance of his tent (Genesis 18:1). However, whilst he was looking out, I am looking in. The roles have been reversed. The guests have become the hosts. The people to whom Abraham offered hospitality are now inviting me to come and join them. I stand hovering in the doorway. I see the empty space. Will I step forward and take my place at the table?

If I do, I can then go on to imagine the conversation which follows. What do I bring to the table? What am I carrying in my bag or my luggage that I want to share? What do the Holy Trinity say to me? How do I respond? Do I laugh like Sarah? Do I cry?

For me, that imaginary conversation is prayer. It is where two rivers meet: the river of my longing and desire for communion with God, and the river of God's longing and desire for communion with me. Sometimes, no words are exchanged. Our body language—the focus of our gaze, the bowing of our head, the positioning of our hands and feet—says it all. That is also prayer. And even if I do not come to the table but remain hesitantly on the threshold, that too is prayer.

When I lived in Moscow as a student from 1991–2, we frequently used to go to Pizza Hut. This would have been an unaffordable luxury for the average Russian but was reasonably priced for people like us who had American dollars. I remember sitting at a table by the window one day. The waiter had just brought our pizzas, when I suddenly became aware of the face of a little boy pressed up right against the window. His jaw had dropped, and there was a look of wonder and delight on his face as he stared at our pizzas. Thankfully, he was also coming into the restaurant with his mother. His joyful anticipation as he saw what awaited him reminded me of the feelings which can arise in me as I gaze at an icon or stand on the threshold of some other form of prayer.

In Paragraph 75 of his Spiritual Exercises, Ignatius of Loyola gives the following advice:

> A step or two in front of the place where I am to contemplate or meditate, I will stand for the length of an Our Father, raising my mind above and considering how God our Lord is looking at me, etc., and make an act of reverence or humility.

That is what the little boy in Moscow was doing as he looked though the Pizza Hut window. That is what both hosts and guests do as they approach the door and prepare to meet the person on the other side. That is what prayer does. Stand a short distance away and gaze at the fellowship—the communion—into which you are invited. Then, draw closer and take your place in the hospitable space where the river of your life and the river of God's life meet.

4

Mary gets evangelized

September 2004

On Friday 3 September, I went with some of our church youth group to see Mel Gibson's The Passion of the Christ *at the local cinema. We came home and turned on the television only to find ourselves facing more blood and violence as we were informed of the horrendous outcome of the school siege in Beslan. 186 children lost their lives. This morning, as I stood to preach to our congregation on the parables of loss in Chapter 15 of Luke's Gospel, their eyes turned to me with a desperate searching gaze. "Help us to believe," I felt them saying, "that it is only the fool who says in his heart that there is no God" (Psalm 14:1).*

We have been deeply touched by the messages that have come from around the world over the last ten days assuring us of your heartfelt compassion for Mother Russia and your loving prayers for her children. Your emails also helped me to get a clearer picture of what had actually happened as the media reports here were initially very restrained. One television channel in particular is so controlled by the Government that the first part of every news bulletin simply informs us what President Putin has been doing that day. Pskov can also feel very remote from the rest of this huge country. Many people have never been to Moscow—let alone the Northern Caucasus—and it is naively assumed that a terrorist attack could never happen here. Over the summer holidays I delivered some net curtains to Galya's mother at the school where they both work. I was amazed to be able to walk into the building with a large bag over my shoulder and make my way to the deputy head's office without being challenged by anyone.

There is not a week that goes by without the Methodist presence in Pskov being challenged in some way. We hit the headlines ourselves in late August when a half-page article about the construction of our new church building was published in the Pskov edition of Argumenty i Fakty—one of the most widely read newspapers in Russia. Ten days after the article appeared, we were informed that the premises we rent would no longer be available to us and that we were to come immediately and collect all the hymnbooks etc. that we store there. Thankfully, we have been able to return to the Music School where the church originally met, but we have to gather very secretly, keeping our altar cross and dog collars etc. well concealed until we are safely inside the building.

Our new Bible study group in Ostrov—a neighbouring town—was launched recently. We had only just arrived when one of the neighbours ran out of her house and stared shouting that no one should associate with us *because we were a dangerous sect. We were concerned that she had already frightened any prospective members away, but four women (and two dogs!) came to share in fellowship with us and are keen for us to return.*

Steve Rosenberg, the current BBC Russia editor, has a wonderful YouTube channel which features recordings of his own brilliant piano playing and a series of short film clips from Valentina's kiosk. The kiosk is as close as you can get in Russia to a British newsagent's shop. Valentina sells newspapers and magazines, crossword and puzzle books, toys and calendars. When I first visited Russia in the 1980s, I can only remember seeing two newspapers—*Pravda* (meaning "truth") and *Izvestiya* (meaning "news")—which were pasted on billboards for people to read on the street. There used to be a Soviet joke about these papers which said that there was no News in the Truth and no Truth in the News! Now, as can be seen at Valentina's kiosk, there is a vast array of different publications to choose from—even if many of them are controlled or owned by the Russian Government.

The news programme I refer to in the extract from my letter above is called *Vesti* which is the root word of *Izvestiya* and means "news". The Russian or, more accurately, Church Slavonic, word for the Annunciation is *Blagoveshcheniye*, which also has *vesti* at its core and literally means the "good-newsing". In Greek, the icon pictured above is called *Evangelismos*, which also means "good news" and is where we get the word evangelism from. Hence the title of this chapter.

When I was a student in Moscow from 1991–2, there seemed to be evangelists on every street corner. The Soviet Union was falling apart, and it was not just alternative newspapers which started appearing. Outside the metro stations, there were stalls selling New Testaments piled alongside copies of the Quran, the Communist Manifesto, the Bhagavadgita and collections of horoscopes. I remember wondering how people who had been taught for so long that there was only one path to follow could suddenly make an informed choice about the multiple philosophies and beliefs that were now on offer. I also got very frustrated with the American missionaries who thought they were bringing the light of Christ to Russia and seemed oblivious to the fact that in 988, Prince Vladimir of Kyiv, the grandson of Princess Olga who founded the city of Pskov, ordered a mass baptism of the people of the lands then known as Rus—over five hundred years before Christopher Columbus sailed the ocean blue.

You may therefore be wondering why I felt it was right and appropriate to go and be a mission partner myself ten years later. You will already have gathered from what I have written above that the way in which we choose and use words is fascinating and important to me. Being a mission partner is not the same as being a missionary. Nor is it the same as being an evangelist. In 1995, the Methodist Church in Britain deliberately chose to stop using the term missionary—which was associated with our colonial past—and to start using the term mission partner. The word partner is key here. People are no longer sent somewhere simply because the British Church thinks that another country needs what we can bring. Mission partners work with our partner churches around the world at the invitation of those churches. That includes people from other countries serving in Britain. It is also now quite rare for mission partners to serve overseas for life. It is important for mission partners to return and offer to the home church the learning and the insights which have been received overseas. We no longer assume that we have everything to give and nothing to receive. We now recognize that this is about partnership and relationship. Both host and guest—as we saw in the last chapter—have something to bring to the table.

It would take a whole book to explore the relationship between mission and evangelism. I will simply say that, for me, mission is much broader than evangelism. I do not see them as two rivers. I see evangelism as a river and mission as the lake into which evangelism flows. I would like to suggest that these first two icons in the festival row are primarily about evangelism. They are about angels—messengers—bringing good news. The evangelist gives. The evangelized receives. The icons we will go on to look at are, in my view, more focused on mission. They are about worship, foot-washing, myrrh-bearing, finding God in birth and death and in the bustle of city life.

Mary gets evangelized! She does not get much choice about it—which is what used to annoy me about the American missionaries in Moscow who would preach to people who were stuck in a long queue. Those people were a captive audience. So was Mary. Gabriel did not ask if he could come and talk to her. He just appeared and then immediately launched into his announcement of good news. I am not sure how good the news that she was pregnant and that her boyfriend was not the father would have felt to teenage Mary. Her response to this evangelism and her acceptance of her role in God's mission is remarkable. She does not have the bolshie attitude I had when I was fourteen and did not want to do what Mr Dewey was asking of me! Mary said: "Here am I, the servant of the Lord; let it be with me according to your word" (Luke 1:38).

Despite the many ways in which I differ from Mary, I do also feel a deep sense of connection with her. We are both mission partners—saying yes to a call from God which will take us to a place we have never been before. We were both teenagers when we became aware of a stirring (both inner and outer) to which we needed to be attentive. We both carry the word of God within us and, through our labours, that word is delivered. We are both aware that the life we love and the love we live are given by God and not something we could have conceived of ourselves.

If I could create my own festival row, I would definitely want to include an icon of the Visitation—the meeting between Elizabeth and Mary which immediately follows the Annunciation (Luke 1:39–45). I have a beautiful depiction of this encounter in my home which was painted for me by a friend as an ordination present. For me, this is a moment where two rivers meet and, in fact, in my friend's painting there is a river behind the two women, into or out of which they both seem to flow.

If we see Mary as a river, then we can see Gabriel and Elizabeth as the riverbanks, holding Mary and helping to shape and form and direct her as she discerns and follows her path. I thank God for all the people in my life who have done for me what Gabriel and Elizabeth did for Mary. Some of them have already died and crossed over to the other side. Others I have yet to meet but will discover as my journey continues. All these people are the banks of my river who continually support and re-source me.

I started this chapter by talking about the Russian press. In Britain, we can also get a very different view or interpretation of an event depending which newspaper we read. To some extent, the same is true of the Gospel writers. Luke is the only Gospel writer who includes an account of the Annunciation and the Visitation. It is normally assumed that Mary must have been the source of this material, but it would be interesting to know how accurate Mary and Gabriel and Elizabeth thought Luke's write-up was! In Mikhail Bulgakov's wonderful novel

The Master and Margarita, Ieshua (the Jesus character) expresses his concern about the inaccuracy of what Matvei-Levi is writing about him: "One day I looked at his parchment and was horrified. Absolutely nothing of what is written there was said by me. I begged him: Burn your parchment, for God's sake. But he snatched it from my hands and ran away" (Chapter 2, my translation).

Here is an extract (again my own translation) from the newspaper article I referred to above which was published whilst I was living in Pskov:

> In an interview with *Pskovskaya Pravda* (a local newspaper), Georgy Drachev, head of the Pskov region's FSB (formerly the KGB), reported that foreign religious organizations often "approach families of military personnel and relatives of officials who work for intelligence agencies or have access to state secrets" and that "many of these so-called 'preachers' were trained in Western secret service camps". Acknowledging that "the religious organizations represented in the Pskov region (Mormons, Jehovah's Witnesses, Pentecostalists, Baptists, Seventh Day Adventists, Methodists and others) operate legally", he declared that it was necessary to counteract these "destructive" organizations. "If you or one of your relatives has become part of a sect and this has resulted in a worsening of relationships within the family, a decline

> in physical or mental health, or pressure to
> hand over property, get in touch with the law
> enforcement agencies."

I did not recognize myself or my colleagues from other denominations in this description, and it was frightening to realize that this is how the average person in the street might see me. My time in Russia made me very aware that what one person declares as gospel truth can be viewed with equal conviction as fake news by someone else. That has an impact on the way in which we engage in mission and evangelism. In a May 2019 conversation at St Paul's Cathedral about her book *Holy Envy: Finding God in the Faith of Others*, Barbara Brown Taylor was asked a question about how we do evangelism in the context of our engagement with people of other faiths. She said: "If you are going into a conversation intent on conversion, are you open to being converted yourself?"

Little Window 1

The little windows (*okoshki*) through which business is normally conducted in Russia—purchasing train tickets, submitting documents, changing money, posting letters—often close for a "technical break". The times of these breaks are indicated on each window, but it is not always easy to tell when you join the queue if you will be served before the next break comes. This is the first of two little windows in this book. Please feel free to take a tea break!

Registering in your hometown

December 2004

Every Christmas the opening verses of the second chapter of Luke's Gospel are read in church, and we are reminded that Joseph had to travel to his hometown of Bethlehem to register for the census and that Mary, in the late stages of her pregnancy, went with him. Before coming to live and work as a mission partner in Russia I had never seriously considered what that registration process might involve. What follows is an account of what Mary and Joseph would have had to go through if Bethlehem had been a Russian town!

Firstly, they would have to gather numerous documents. These would have to be original copies with official signatures and stamps. At least two of each would be required. If the wording was not acceptable, they would be sent back to Nazareth to start all over again.

Secondly, they would have to carry with them a large amount of cash in order to pay all the fees, bribes and the cost of travel, food and accommodation along the way. If none of this cash was stolen by pickpockets en route, it could still be rejected by the cashier as being too crumpled and creased.

Thirdly, they would have to converse with bureaucrats not only in bureaucratic language but in a language which was not their native tongue. This would be tiring, confusing and stressful.

Fourthly, there would be queues everywhere, with people constantly trying to push in and long hours spent standing and waiting with no toilet or refreshment facilities.

All of this has been my experience recently whilst trying to register my visa in my hometown of Pskov. I now have a deeper empathy for Mary and Joseph, and I am left wondering whether they managed to complete all the paperwork before Jesus was born. Presumably, they would then have been required to fill in countless forms to register his birth and perhaps even go through the whole process again to include this newborn child in the census!

5

A parent's sacrifice

A prayer written by Mollie Priest (my mother) for the *Methodist Prayer Handbook 2005–6*:

> Generous God, my daughter
>   responded to an invitation,
> in your name, to journey to Russia.
> This fills me with pride at her deep faith,
> boundless courage and linguistic skills.
> Yet, her absence, Lord, is a thief to my joy.
> I am wrapped in moments of emptiness
> as I miss her laughter, visits and shared outings.
> Her journey has a purpose.
> Fill her with an attitude of mission.
> Fill me with gentleness of spirit.
> Her journey has obstacles.
> Fill her with strength and patience for each crisis.
> Fill me with grace to support her in the struggle.
> She journeys with the greatest friend of all.
> Fill all families, separated by barriers of distance,
> with your calming, constant presence
>   in our lives. Amen.*

*   First published in the 2005/2006 *Methodist Prayer Handbook*, © Trustees for Methodist Church Purposes, reproduced with permission.

I should probably have asked my mother to write this chapter. Fewer than three years had passed since the death of my father when I got on a plane and flew to live in Russia. That felt like another bereavement for my mum—another empty place at the table for Christmas and other family gatherings. She can no doubt identify profoundly with Mary in this icon. The sacrifice being made here is not only the two turtle doves or pigeons which Joseph has brought but the sacrifice which Mary makes in letting go of her child. In handing him over to Simeon, she is, in a sense, handing him over to death. This is the place where birth and death meet. The old man looks into the eyes of the newborn baby and knows that he can now depart in peace. Mary goes home, knowing that her love for this child will bring her piercing pain as well as overwhelming joy (Luke 2:28–35).

This icon reminds me of an episode in the BBC hospital drama *Casualty* when a new mother is told that there is a 50 per cent chance of her baby developing Huntingdon's disease—a fatal genetic disorder. The child cannot be tested until he is eighteen years old, and so this mother is faced with living with that uncertain knowledge for a long time. That news—to borrow some words from my mother's prayer—is a thief to her joy.

One of the most famous icons of Mary is the *Vladimir Virgin of Tenderness* which is housed in the church at the Tretyakov Gallery in Moscow. It depicts Mary holding an adult-looking Christ child. His head is resting against her cheek, and his arm is wrapped around her neck. Mary's face is turned towards the viewer, and she looks desperately sad.

Friends who visited me in Russia would often ask in the first day or two whether Russians ever smile. Behind closed doors, with friends around the kitchen table, there is plenty of joy and laughter—but it is rare to see happy faces on icons or on the street. An American friend, who came to Pskov regularly, made it his mission every day to try to get a smile from a shop assistant or a bus conductor.

I think I was drawn to Russian and Russia partly because of the depth of suffering which I associated with the people and the place. My most profound experiences of God have come at times of pain and loss. My spirituality is rooted in a crucified God, and I can be quite dismissive of those who seem to focus on the triumph of Easter Day without having plumbed the depths of Good Friday. That does not mean that I do not believe in the resurrection. It does mean that, like Thomas, I need to see the wounds of Christ before I can find healing and hope (John 20:25).

Galya, my flatmate in Pskov, used to get frustrated when I wanted to spend the evening watching a gloomy dramatization of a Dostoevsky novel and she wanted to watch a comedy show. "We Russians don't need any more Dostoevsky," she said. "We have had enough pain and suffering. We need to laugh now." I was interested to discover that there is a Russian word (*khokhotun*—masculine, *khokhotushka*—feminine) for someone who laughs a lot which, as far as I know, has no direct equivalent in English. I suppose we would call someone a giggler, but the Russian word could be translated as a giggle-box—the laughing version of a chatterbox!

I think that Anna—the other woman in the icon—was probably both a giggle-box and a chatterbox. She had had her share of sorrow. Her husband had died after only seven years of marriage (Luke 2:36–8), but she seems full of life and enthusiasm in the temple. Simeon and Mary have this deep, intense conversation (as you might find in a Dostoevsky novel!) whilst Anna goes around bubbling with infectious joy and telling everyone about Jesus.

I have to confess that Anna also reminds me of some of the women you can find today in Russian Orthodox churches—cleaning the candle stands and keeping a close eye on everyone who comes through the door. I was once told off by one such woman because she felt the split in the back of my skirt was an attempt to seduce the priest. I also frequently observed older women like Anna telling young parents in the street, whom they had never met before, that their child was either overdressed or underdressed for the weather. I remember getting rebuked myself for sitting on a wall in the summer, because, this woman insisted, my ovaries would get frozen.

This icon is where two rivers meet: laughter and tears, age and youth, birth and death. The Russian title of the icon—*Sreteniye*—is an archaic word which means "meeting" or "encounter". Rather like the icon of the Old Testament Trinity, there is also a space for us in this meeting place. We can perhaps imagine ourselves stepping forward and stretching out our arms to receive Jesus from Mary.

The structures behind the people remind us that this encounter is taking place in the temple—a place where one expects to meet with God. The temple plays a significant role in Luke's Gospel—the only Gospel to include this particular episode in Jesus' life. Luke both begins and ends his Gospel in the temple (Luke 1:8–9; 24:53).

For me, this icon suggests that our life—like Luke's Gospel—is framed and held by our place of worship. I was carried into church for baptism at the beginning of my life, and I will be carried into church for my funeral when my earthly life has come to an end. In between those two significant events, I keep returning to this meeting place with God in order to present to God what I am carrying—as Mary and Joseph presented Jesus.

As I look at this icon, I wonder what I need to offer today, what I need to let go of, what I need to receive. It seems to me that there is a longing and an ache in all four adults in the icon both to give and to receive. They are all leaning forward with arms outstretched—some with hands empty, others with hands full. Such posture and intent also remind me of the sacrament of Holy Communion. Simeon has stretched out his hands to receive the body of Christ, and I see Mary here as the priest, offering Christ to him.

There is a physicality in this encounter which goes beyond the physical structure of the temple. It is a physicality which goes beyond our bodies and pierces our souls. That is what worship—especially sacramental worship—can do. The ordinary gifts of the earth—water, bread, wine—touch us both physically and spiritually. What we feel in our bodies, we also feel in our souls.

Body and soul appeared in the list I gave in Chapter 2 of the various pairings of rivers which find a meeting place within me. I am aware of the intimate relationship between spirituality and sexuality. Making love is another experience where what we feel in our bodies, we also feel in our souls. And yet the Church has often tried to keep body and soul apart. One of the reasons why Mary had come to the temple was for the rites of purification. She would have been seen as unclean for forty days after childbirth, and the sacrifice of the two turtle doves or pigeons would have enabled her to be pronounced clean again (Leviticus 12:1–8). That is just one example of a religious viewpoint which sees the body as sinful whilst the soul is pure.

This meeting in the temple affirms for me that when body and soul meet, we are on holy ground. As Simeon physically holds the baby in his arms, he has a spiritual experience; he sees salvation. In the previous icon of the

Annunciation, Mary had a spiritual experience which affected her body. She was penetrated by the Holy Spirit and went on to experience the visceral physicality of pregnancy and childbirth. Body and soul are deeply connected. These two rivers need to meet.

I am writing this book during a sabbatical which I had hoped to spend in Pskov. The COVID-19 pandemic made that impossible. I have appreciated being able to connect with my friends in Russia through internet video calls, but this is not the same as being physically present. This virtual world we have been living in has made the incarnation even more important to me. The Word became flesh (John 1:14). That is what I try to live out and model in my ministry—and I think this is particularly important for mission partners. Mission partners embody the partnership and relationship between different churches, cultures and countries.

I once heard an amusing anecdote about someone who asked a computer to translate the biblical quote "The spirit is willing, but the flesh is weak" (Matthew 26:41) into Russian. This was the result: "The vodka is strong, but the meat is rotten"! We can laugh about that, but it does also remind us that the call to follow Christ can be costly and demanding on our bodies.

In the Richmond Room at Methodist Church House in London, there are four boards listing the name, place of service, year of entry and year of death of the 125 missionaries who trained at Richmond College between 1840 and 1950. Almost half of them died within ten years of entering college—mostly from some form of fever. I am not sure if I would have offered to serve overseas if the risk of premature death was still so high. I knew that I could come back to Britain quickly and easily if I did develop any health problems.

I developed bronchitis during my first Russian winter. At the time, I was living in an apartment owned by the church. I was rather perturbed when one church member (who had a key to the apartment) marched into my bedroom and announced that she was going to put *kartoshki v mundirakh* on my chest. I understood this to mean potatoes in their military uniforms. It turned out she was referring to hot jacket potato skins which were actually very effective.

Another new experience for me was going to see a gynaecologist to get a certificate stating that I could use the public swimming pool. This visit eventually led to me having a hysterectomy at the Royal London Hospital in Whitechapel some years later. I hasten to add that this was not because of what the Russian gynaecologist did to me! I ended up feeling grateful to her for discovering some issues of which I would have been blissfully unaware if I had not wanted to go swimming.

On a more positive note, the NHS dentist I signed up with on my return to the UK was impressed by the white filling—costing the equivalent of £10—which the private dentist I went to in Pskov had done for me. My optician in Pskov assured me that he was the most

Western optician in Russia—but this turned out to be a geographical rather than a technological claim!

I also managed to break my wrist—whilst rollerblading with my friend Yulia. Yulia took me to the *traumpunkt* (emergency room) where the bone had to be manipulated back into place. As we were waiting to be called into the plaster room, I received a text from my mum: "Are you ok?" she wrote. "I can hear you crying." My mum is incredibly intuitive, and this was not the first time she had known that something was wrong with me before I had told her. This was another example of two rivers meeting. Her soul, like Mary's, was pierced by my physical pain.

6

The Passion of Pushkin

May 2005

The whole place looked more like a village fete than an Orthodox Church just hours away from the great Easter Liturgy. People stood beside a long row of trestle tables, carefully arranging the decorated eggs and kulich *(iced fruit bread) with which they would break their Easter fast the following morning. They were waiting for the priest to come and bless this festive food, but he was currently otherwise engaged. Outside in the courtyard stood a clapped-out Lada with its doors, bonnet and boot open. This was where the priest was—dousing the car with incense and holy water. He was reading from a prayer book, so there is obviously a special liturgy for such occasions. It was certainly an appropriate day on which to conduct this rite for a vehicle so clearly in need of resurrection.*

I returned to the church shortly before midnight, having been to my German class in the meantime. Svetlana, our church choir director and the wife of my teacher, accompanied me. Standing on tiptoe we managed to get

*a glimpse into the church where the congregation was
standing in silence before the closed doors of the altar.
We joined a queue to buy candles and found a space with
a good view opposite the main church doors. We were
surrounded by hundreds of (young) people. Up in the
bell tower tolled the solitary solemn sound of death. When
it got to 12:10 a.m., and there was still no movement,
Svetlana commented that, since we had already changed
the clocks, we may have another hour to wait. It was
possible that the Orthodox Church was not only working
to a different calendar but to a different time of day.
However, a few minutes later, all the bells suddenly began
to peal with exuberant joy and the procession began. With
lanterns, banners, icons and radiant vestments and song,
the choir, priests and people made a full circle of the
church and graveyard which took about twenty minutes.
The main door, which had been closed once the church
had emptied, was reopened to reveal a blaze of light inside
as the Easter acclamation was repeatedly proclaimed:*
Christos voskres! Vo istinu voskres! *(Christ is risen! He
is risen indeed!)*

The Russian word for Sunday is *Voskreseniye*, which
is almost identical to the word for resurrection. I love
the fact that, when it was forbidden to celebrate Easter
during the Communist period, Russians were still aware
that every week had a day of resurrection.

It is traditional in Russia for the funeral and burial
to take place on the third day because Jesus was dead

for three days before rising again. I remember Nelli, my colleague in Pskov, receiving news that her father was very weak and probably coming to the end of his life. He was several thousand kilometres away in the Urals, and there was no guarantee that she would get there in time. Her father died just half an hour before Nelli got to the end of her three-day train journey from Pskov.

Jesus did not leave immediately when he heard that his friend, Lazarus, was ill. He stayed where he was for two more days (John 11:6). By the time he arrived in Bethany, Lazarus had already been in the tomb for four days (John 11:17). Not surprisingly, Mary and Martha were both upset that Jesus had not come earlier. They both—separately—said to him: "Lord, if you had been here, my brother would not have died" (John 11:21,32).

My father, who was also a Methodist minister, taught me that if you are informed that someone is dying, you should go immediately because, otherwise, it might be too late. Saying our goodbyes is really important. One of the hardest parts of the COVID-19 pandemic was that it was rarely possible for relatives to be with their loved ones as they died.

Some of the most difficult moments in my ministry have been when people have told me how hurt they were by my absence in their time of need. Weeping with them—as Jesus wept in Bethany (John 11:35)—has sometimes been the only response I could make.

I have also shed tears in my personal life when men I have loved were not present—physically or emotionally—when I desperately needed them to be. I was—and remain—profoundly affected by the heart-wrenching scene at the end of the 1999 film *Onegin*, starring Ralph Fiennes (whom I admit I had a crush on!) in the title role. The film is based on *Eugene Onegin*, a novel in verse written by the famous Russian poet Alexander Pushkin. If you are unfamiliar with this story, I apologize for the spoilers which follow.

The four main characters are two sisters (Olga and Tatiana), a man who dies (Lensky), and a man who causes pain by not responding sooner (Onegin). The grand climax of the film shows Onegin meeting with Tatiana. When they were younger, Tatiana had fallen passionately in love with Onegin, but he had rejected her. Years later, after she has married someone else, they meet again. Onegin realizes the mistake he has made, but Tatiana tells him that he is too late. For me, her cry of anguish not only echoes my own experience but also the cry of Martha and Mary when Jesus finally appears.

Onegin's lateness is a recurrent theme in the novel. The story begins with Onegin receiving news that his uncle is dying and would be glad to say farewell to him. He sets off immediately but, by the time he arrives, his uncle has already died (Chapter 1, Stanza 52). He arrives late to Tatiana's name-day party (Chapter 5, Stanza 29) and is even late to the duel in which he kills his friend, Lensky (Chapter 6, Stanza 24).

I have also been struck by other parallels between Pushkin's novel in verse and the story of Jesus' relationship with Mary, Martha and Lazarus. Like the novel, the Gospel story has four main characters: two sisters (Martha and Mary), a man who dies (Lazarus), and a man who causes pain by not responding sooner (Jesus).

Pushkin describes Onegin and Lensky as "water and stone, poetry and prose, ice and flame" (Chapter 2, Stanza 13). In Luke's Gospel, Mary and Martha are also depicted as having contrasting characters and personalities. Martha gets cross that Mary is sitting at Jesus' feet whilst she is doing all the work (Luke 10:38–42). Likewise, Tatiana and her sister Olga are very different. Tatiana really reminds me of Mary of Bethany. She is a reflective, dreamy type with a rich inner life who loves to read and immerse herself in another world (Chapter 2, Stanzas 25–9).

I also see myself in Tatiana, which is probably why I find her experience so poignant. She first expresses her love for Onegin by writing him a letter. I fell in love with someone by exchanging long poetic, passionate airmail letters when I was a student in Moscow, but I discovered that words do not always become flesh. After a later relationship also left me feeling broken and damaged, I learnt through psychotherapy that I need to let go of the fantasy I have created in my imagination and engage with reality.

I love the way in which this icon holds together the reality of human life with an event which must have seemed like supernatural fiction. The man holding his nose because of the stench reminds us that dealing with human bodies can be messy and unpleasant. The men who have lifted away the stone from the tomb are clearly finding it very heavy. Mary and Martha seem so tiny and fragile as they kneel before Jesus. The religious leaders looking on are taller than everybody else as if they have put themselves on a pedestal. Jesus' disciples seem to be hiding behind him, like children clinging to their mother's knees. And then there is Lazarus, tightly bound except for his face, and presumably struggling to comprehend what has happened to him.

When Onegin goes to visit Tatiana at the end of the novel, Pushkin describes him as "similar to a corpse" (Chapter 8, Stanza 40). He moves through the palace without meeting a single living soul, until he opens a door and finds Tatiana. Onegin is hoping for resurrection, but it is Tatiana who experiences that instead. Pushkin writes that as Tatiana looks at Onegin, "that simple young girl with the dreams and heart of former days has now risen again (*voskresla*) within her" (Chapter 8, Stanza 41). Lazarus was unbound from his grave clothes (John 11:44), but both Tatiana and Onegin are doomed to spend the rest of their lives wrapped in the knowledge that the happiness which had once seemed so close and possible is now unattainable.

Tchaikovsky wrote an opera based on Eugene Onegin, which I first saw at the Bolshoi Theatre in 1992. On the rare occasions when it is staged in Britain, I always try to get a ticket, and I intend to have Lensky's aria played at my funeral. The 2013 Royal Opera House production really brought home to me that our past is something which remains with us. The director, Kasper Holten, aware that Pushkin tells the story in the past tense, chose to start by showing Onegin arriving for his final meeting with Tatiana, and the opera then played out as if these two characters were looking back on their life. Holten used two creative devices to express physically the inner emotion of the characters as they relived their memories.

The first was that two dancers sometimes appeared on stage as doubles of the singers. This enabled the mature characters to watch their younger selves. The clothes for the younger and mature characters were identifiably the same, but layers were added as the characters got older. This reminded me of a Russian *matrëshka* (nesting doll). Our past is buried deep within us, and there are times when we, like Lazarus, find the layers are being removed and we meet again the person we were before.

The second was that "souvenirs" were left on stage as visual reminders of the emotional baggage which Onegin and Tatiana were carrying. This started fairly innocuously with a sheaf of wheat brought in from the field by the peasants in the opening scene but culminated in Lensky's dead body remaining on stage after the duel until the end of the opera—another two scenes. This was an incredibly powerful reminder of how major events from our past are always present in our lives.

The grief which follows the death of a significant person in our life is a prime example of this. During the COVID-19 pandemic, I did some training with Cruse Bereavement Care. We were introduced to a model of grief developed by Lois Tonkin. This model was illustrated by a shaded circle to indicate how initially our grief takes over the whole of our life. With time, another circle emerges around the grief as our life continues, but the shaded circle in the centre is always there.

I have always wondered what it must have been like for Lazarus to die and come back to life again—and presumably to die again later. And yet, in a sense, all our lives are made up of a series of little deaths and little resurrections. We constantly experience losses and new discoveries, hellos and goodbyes. We can relate to Pushkin's characters because we also know what it is like to have two rivers meet within us—our younger and older selves, fantasy and reality, dreams and regrets. The problem comes when these rivers freeze—as the rivers in Pskov did every winter—and prevent us from moving forward. Then, like Lazarus who was immobilized by his grave clothes, we need someone to come and unbind us and let us go.

Little Window 2

Holy Week

March 2005

It was at 6:20 a.m. when the Pskov train entered the city of Moscow. The platform was already crowded with porters and taxi drivers, waving signs and shouting "Hotels, Hotels". I set off to meet Bishop Växby—the one who had recently come to serve Eurasia in the name of the Lord. The stones were crying out as the builders continued to work on this new location for the office and seminary.

On Monday, the builders of the Methodist Church in Pskov were sacked. They had been deceiving the people with their own rates of exchange and their disrespectful attitude to this house of prayer. The tables were turned on them as a new firm appeared to take their place.

On Tuesday, there was weeping and wailing as two sisters in Christ grieved. One had travelled to the funeral of her father only to find that her mother had also died by the time she got there. Another was facing the terminal illness of the man she loved. "If you had been here, my brother would not have died," they said. But were these words of reproach (if God was truly with us, we would not be facing such suffering) or of affirmation (where God is, death is not)?

On Wednesday, the Church Council met. There was conflict in the ranks—and the one who controlled the purse strings was made to feel the blame. Are others to dictate to us how we can spend our money, or are we free to make our own decisions? There was a costly outpouring of tears.

On Thursday, the youth group met in an upper room to break bread together as their Lent course on the film Chocolat *drew to a close. A new understanding of what it means to be "church" challenged our relationships both around and beyond the table.*

On Friday, pushed and shoved into public transport with arms stretched out to grasp the handrail, two thieves—one on either side—went about their business. Loss, fear, vulnerability, powerlessness were all part of the St Peter(sburg) experience.

On Saturday, there was time for reflection as we sat in the waiting room between the past and the future. Conscious of what had brought us to this point, we tried to discern appropriate ways forward. Baggage was unpacked. Some things were left behind whilst others were carefully wrapped up again to continue their journey.

Overnight, the ice on the river began to crack and the waters of new life broke. Clothes which people had buried themselves in against the deathly cold were neatly folded away. Those who had carried their skis onto the bus now appeared with gardening tools. And amidst the smell of incense, bells began to ring as bread was broken and the Word of the Lord echoed through the graveyard: Christ is risen!

7

Entering the city

August 2010

The Patriarch (the most high-ranking bishop of the Russian Orthodox Church) had come to town. When I went downtown to register my visa, the buses were all being diverted, and I had to pass through a security check as I walked up October Street to Lenin Square. An old man walked past me muttering to himself: "The Communists closed the streets for their processions. Now the church is closing the streets!" There was a two-hour wait before the Patriarch was due to appear, and I did not hang around. I had only slept a few hours the previous night, having arrived in Pskov at 3 a.m.

I had booked a flight to Pskov via Riga with Baltic Air, but the Pskov leg later got cancelled. This was probably because the Patriarch's private plane landed at Pskov Airport that same night. Two friends met me at Riga Airport and drove me though Latvia and Estonia and across the Russian border to Pskov. I think this is the first time I have been in four countries in one day. We sat in a queue of vehicles at the Russian border for several hours.

"It seems that the Motherland is not awaiting us," said Dima. Sergei had fallen asleep in the front passenger seat. The man in the car behind us came up and asked: "Why is he asleep?" "Because he's tired!" said Dima.

I always get nervous at the Russian border, and, as usual, I got told off. My visa application had been rejected the first time around because I had written that I would be staying at a private address rather than a hotel. The woman at the visa centre said that if I got the papers reissued to reflect this, then everything would be perfect. I returned with amended documents a week later only to find that the woman on duty that morning was not bothered about where I was staying. She did, however, want to know the phone number of the bookshop where I had worked in 1993 and the name of my manager. When filling in my migration form at the border, I had taken care to put the full address of where I was staying, but the immigration officer crossed it out and shouted at me: "Why have you put all that? Just write 'Pskov' next time!"

The Russian visa application process involves having your fingerprints scanned. Last time I went through this, the man behind the desk asked, "Are you nervous?" This only increased the anxiety I feel whenever I place my papers into the hands of a Russian bureaucrat. I began to wonder whether the machine on which my fingers were resting was also a lie detector. "Why would I be nervous?" I said, in as relaxed a tone as my inner panic would allow. "Because some people think Russia is a scary place," he responded. "Oh no!" I replied. "I've been to Russia lots of times, and I'm really excited to be going back again." "Take a seat. I need to call the Embassy," he said. The next few minutes felt like several weeks as I waited for him to return and summon me back to the desk again. "Everything is in order," he said. "You can collect your visa next week." I thanked him in my best Russian and emerged onto the street feeling both exhilarated and exhausted.

This emotional rollercoaster which I ride each time I go to Russia is similar, I suspect, to the mixed emotions which Jesus was feeling as he rode into Jerusalem. Nerves and excitement, trepidation and triumph, and a deep sense that his life and his future were now dependent on people whose initial response to him would not necessarily be the same a few days later.

If the Palm Sunday narrative was set in contemporary Russia, then I think Jesus would arrive in the city on an overnight train. My vision of this may well be influenced by the photos and paintings I have seen of Lenin arriving in April 1917 at the Finland Station in what was then known as Petrograd (now St Petersburg). This was Lenin's re-entry into Russia after a period of exile in Western Europe. He stood on top of a train carriage to address the crowds who had gathered to welcome him and declared his intention to lead a revolution, transferring power from the Government to the proletariat (working-class people).

When I think about what it means and feels like to enter a city, I immediately think of trains. I have many memories from my time in Russia of being woken up in the early morning by the attendant in charge of the train carriage. Bio toilets have now been introduced on most trains, but previously the toilets emptied onto the track. This necessitated a "sanitary zone" around each station which meant that the toilets would be locked half an hour before arriving in the city. Allowing time for everyone to use the facilities necessitated early wake-up calls. I have fond memories of those half-hour periods afterwards as everyone sat on their bunks, drinking tea and recovering from the rude and rushed awakening. That was the time when interesting conversations with the strangers you had spent the night with might occur. I also loved the excitement of knowing that we were nearly there, as I looked through the window and saw that tower blocks had now replaced the birch trees which lined much of the route. Getting off the train, my senses were assailed by the sights, sounds and smells as porters and taxi drivers touted for trade, emotional reunions took place on the platform, and others strode off with purpose to elbow their way onto the crowded public transport.

Pskov is a city, but life there is far slower and calmer than the bustle of Moscow and St Petersburg. Jesus would have been aware of a similar contrast between Galilee and Jerusalem. Entering a large city can be a culture shock. It is also an experience which can leave you feeling small and insignificant amongst the throng of people and tall, important-looking buildings.

The four Gospels all record that Jesus was the centre of attention when he entered the city of Jerusalem. People lined the streets to welcome him. Like Lenin, they were expecting him to lead a revolution. The icon, however, does not show a great crowd. Jesus' disciples are huddled tightly behind him, looking rather fearful and uncertain. On the other side, blocking the gates of the city, is a group of people who I take to be the same religious leaders who were standing on a pedestal in the previous icon, observing the raising of Lazarus. Then there are the two much smaller people—who could perhaps even be children. One is laying a cloak on the road. The other has climbed the tree—perhaps to get a better view or to break off some branches to wave. This reminds me that no one in a crowd is too small or insignificant for Jesus to notice them. Jesus sees Zacchaeus in the tree (Luke 19:1–10) and is aware of the woman who reaches though the mass of bodies to touch the fringe of his cloak (Luke 8:43–8). This is the revolution which Jesus has come to bring—to draw attention to those who are normally ignored or unseen and to raise up those who might otherwise be trampled underfoot.

The toppling of the statue of Bristol slave trader Edward Colston in June 2020 at the end of a Black Lives Matter demonstration reminded me of the Moscow coup in 1991 when protestors pulled down the statue of Felix

Dzerzhinsky who founded the Soviet secret police. I later discovered Dzerzhinsky's statue in a kind of graveyard for other Soviet heroes who had been removed from their pedestals. The revolution which Jesus brought also involved a complete shift in the understanding of who should be held up as an example. That is why he entered the city mounted on a humble donkey instead of a noble horse. "He has brought down the powerful from their thrones and lifted the lowly" (Luke 1:52).

The tension which inevitably precedes such revolution is starkly portrayed by this icon. The two groups on either side of it resemble opposing camps or gangs. I could imagine them starting a physical fight if Jesus was not holding the ground between them. The tree in the centre looks as if it is about to topple over. There is a precarious vulnerability about Jesus too. His head is looking towards the city, but his feet are still turned in the opposite direction. The two rivers which meet here are not calmly flowing into one another. They are crashing and foaming and trying to resist the strong opposing current. And in the middle of all this is a tree.

The tree is outside the city walls and, of course, Jesus' entry into the city was followed a few days later by his expulsion from the city as he was taken to be hung on a cross of wood, beyond the "sanitary zone". One of the "souvenirs" which was left on stage in the Royal Opera House production of *Eugene Onegin* (referred to in Chapter 6) was a huge tree branch. Lensky drags it behind him at the beginning of the scene in which he is killed. The tree symbolizes the countryside in which he had spent his childhood and youth—a life blossoming with love, hope and joy which is now about to be cut down and destroyed.

Anton Chekov's play, *The Cherry Orchard*, ends with the sound of an axe striking a tree in the orchard. This poignant ending is not the work of the director but was included by the playwright in the original text. The play was first performed in 1904—a time when Russia was on the verge of revolution. The destruction of the cherry orchard is a symbol of the old order being removed to make way for a new era and way of life.

The replacement of lines of trees by rows of high-rise tower blocks always strikes me when I make an intercity journey in Russia by road or by train. In England, I currently live in Milton Keynes—a city which has so many trees that it could technically be classed as a forest. Cities need trees. The prominence of the solitary tree in the icon, sandwiched between the high-rise buildings, reminds me of how vital trees are, both inside and outside the city. We are now in a race against time globally to plant more trees than we are destroying.

The period we are living through now is also a time of opposing currents. Change is in the air—just as it was when Jesus entered the city of Jerusalem and when Chekhov wrote his plays. The stirring words which the student Trofimov addresses to Anya, the youngest character in *The Cherry Orchard,* are remarkably relevant for us today:

Just think, Anya: your grandfather, great grandfather and all your ancestors were serf-owners, they owned living souls. Don't you see human beings looking at you from every cherry tree in the orchard, from every leaf, from every trunk? Don't you hear their voices? . . . To own human souls—that has corrupted all of you, those living earlier and those living now, so that your mother, you, your uncle, don't even notice that you are living in debt, at someone else's expense, at the expense of those people, whom you won't allow in beyond your entrance hall . . . We are at least two hundred years behind. We don't have anything at all yet, no fixed attitude to the past, we just philosophize, lament or drink vodka. It's clear that to begin to live in the present, we must first atone for our past, to finish with it, and we can atone for it only by suffering, only by extraordinary, relentless hard work.

(Act Two, my translation).

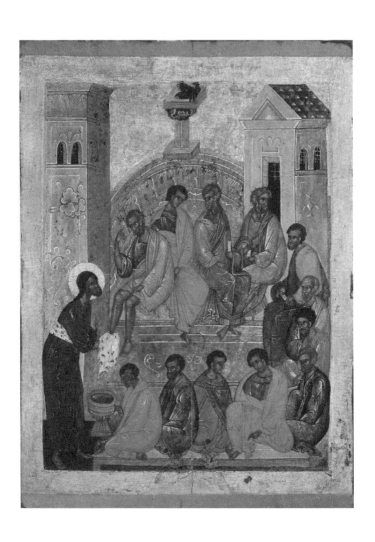

8

Clean Thursday

January 2006

"What are you doing to my people over there?" asked a Zimbabwean friend of mine, following two vicious attacks on black students in St Petersburg. Sadly, racism is rife in Russian society, and these are not isolated incidents. Anyone with a dark skin is usually defined as "one of them" and not "one of us". It was both refreshing and challenging to hear complete strangers described as "my people" in my friend's question; and also, of course, to find myself included in the "you" who were failing to love their neighbours.

Russians have two words for "you". Vy is the formal or plural form (like vous in French), and ty is the informal or singular form (like tu in French). When I first met Kostya, my balalaika teacher, for example, we both addressed each other with the vy form. However, after a few weeks, it became clear that neither of us was quite sure what to do. He is younger than me, and yet he is my teacher. So, the rules were rather confused. We went through a period when he would do anything to avoid using either form of "you". "Have we practised this week?" he would ask. "Yes, we have!" I would reply. Eventually, he just started using the ty *form, and I followed suit.*

On New Year's Eve, I went to a public banya *(bath-house/sauna) for the first time in my life with two members of my English Club. On the way there, one of them explained to me that at the* banya *everyone uses the* ty *form. "Even if you see your boss, whom you would never dream of addressing in that way at work, it's perfectly permissible to do so at the* banya*."*

I recently re-read Zamyatin's We—*a fascinating novel about a Utopian state where people have no concept of an individual "I"—only of a collective "We". Communism obviously engendered a very different sense of community from that which is articulated in the question from my Zimbabwean friend—but I think that "we Brits" have a lot to learn from cultures which talk about "us" rather than about "me".*

When my Russian friend tells me that she was taken to the banya *every Saturday when she was a child because her family lived in a communal apartment where there was only one sink with a cold tap for twenty people, I realize that I know nothing about what it means to share. When my Zimbabwean friend talks about "my people", I realize that I know nothing about what it means to care. When someone who has always addressed me as* vy *takes a risk and suddenly starts using the* ty *form, I realize that I know nothing about what it means to dare.*

May God (who is addressed as Ty *in Russian) keep challenging you and me—which means us—to share, to care and to dare, until the question "What are you doing to my people over there?" no longer needs to be put, because we have learnt what it means to love our neighbour as ourselves.*

There are several names for Maundy Thursday in Russian. Within the Church, it is usually called Holy or Great Thursday. Amongst the general population, it is also known as *chistyy chetverg* which means "Clean Thursday". Since this is the day when Jesus washed the disciples' feet, it has become traditional to go to the *banya* on the Thursday of Holy Week and be cleansed by a good wash and scrub before Easter Day.

When I was first invited to a (private) *banya*, my friends laughed at me when I asked if I would need my swimming costume. "Oh no", they said. "All you need to take is a sheet and a towel." Fortunately, there was not much time to think about what lay ahead of me. Within two hours of the phone call, I was sitting in the steam room with Nelli, the senior pastor, and Rimma, the chair of the church council. There we sat—wearing nothing except a felt hat which helps to insulate your head from the steam. When the heat started making our heads spin, we went back out to the cool "front room", drank tea and smeared our bodies with honey. The climax of the experience—beating each other with birch branches—came an hour or so later, and I emerged feeling invigorated, announcing to my hosts that I would gladly join them there every Saturday night.

The icon of the washing of the feet reminds me of a Russian *banya*. There are normally two benches in the *banya*—one higher (and hotter) than the other. Peter is sitting in what would be the hottest spot—nearest to the stove. He is pointing to his head as he tells Jesus to wash not only his feet but also his hands and his head (John 13:9). However, my irreverent sense of humour as I relate this to the *banya* makes me wonder if he is alerting Jesus that he has not got his felt hat on!

Peter's bare head made me notice for the first time that the disciples do not have halos in this festival row of icons until the final one. I discovered a website which explained that the disciples are often shown without halos in scenes prior to Pentecost. This made sense. The disciples were sanctified with the coming of the Holy Spirit (Acts 2:1–4). I could not understand, however, why Anna and Simeon and the women myrrh-bearers have halos at an earlier stage in the story. I consulted my friend Margaret, a Servite Sister, who has known and loved and prayed with icons for many years. Her interpretation was that Anna, Simeon and the women myrrh-bearers (and, of course, Mary) have already been sanctified because they recognized the truth of the resurrection and of who Christ is much sooner than the twelve male disciples did. I found this insight helpful and illuminating.

The washing of the feet is one of many occasions in the Gospels when the disciples do not understand what Jesus is saying or doing. He is modelling a way of being and relating to others which runs counter to their expectations and culture. I think the Methodist Church in Russia also puzzled and intrigued those who were used to Russian Orthodoxy. Women pastors were a novelty, and the simplicity of the worship space and the worship itself were also strikingly different.

When the possibility of going to serve as a Methodist mission partner in Russia was first suggested to me, I had some serious questions. I felt that Russian Orthodoxy met the needs of the Russian soul, and I was unsure what Methodism would have to offer. I was proved wrong. The Methodist Church does have a role to play in Russia—not least in offering an alternative model in a society where dissenting voices are often silenced. The ideology of Orthodoxy, Autocracy and Nationality which was embraced in the time of Tsar Nicholas I continues to rule Russia today. Putin has now taken the Tsar's place, and the Russian Orthodox Church is seen as being closely aligned with him.

I want to make it quite clear that I do not believe that the Methodist Church is better than the Russian Orthodox Church—or any other denomination. The examples of servant leadership which I am about to give come from the Methodist stable, but I have also been inspired by the Christlike lives and witness of people from many different denominations and traditions. My closest soul friends are Quaker, Anglican and Muslim. I currently serve in the Woughton Ecumenical (Anglican, Methodist, United Reformed and Baptist) Partnership in Milton Keynes, and I am so grateful to the people there for revealing more of God to me. I have already mentioned my dear friend Anne in Paris and her priest, Father (now Bishop) Paul, who made such an impact on me as a teenager. In the next chapter, I will tell you about Father Pavel Adelheim—a Russian Orthodox priest in Pskov. First, let me introduce you to some Methodists.

Eduard Khegay is the current Bishop of the United Methodist Church in Eurasia. The Eurasia Episcopal Area covers the countries of Russia, Belarus, Kazakhstan, Kirghizia, Ukraine and Moldova. Eduard has written a book (only available in Russian) called *Brave and Humble: Christian Leadership in Eurasia*. In the chapter on servant leadership, Eduard recalls that when he was the pastor of a Moscow church, a new African student came to worship there for the first time. Eduard had a chat with him at the lunch table after the service. About a year later, another African student told Eduard how amazed this new student had been when Eduard had brought him a bowl of soup. "I don't get it," he said. "He's the pastor, and yet he served me."

In a later chapter on the character of a leader, Eduard writes this:

> I see my responsibility as a Christian leader to compare my character daily with the character

of Jesus Christ. This is not a simple matter. However, the aim of this exercise is not to see how weak I am, but to see in which direction I should go. In the Methodist Church we call this process "sanctification". Sanctification is our progress in the spiritual life after we have found salvation. Sanctifying grace is poured out on us by our loving God and gives us the strength to understand in which direction we should go and how we can become more Christlike. For this we need to train ourselves to understand the will of God and to carry it out.

(p. 94, my translation).

Eduard is following the example of another brave and humble leader who served the Methodist Church in St Petersburg from 1908–31. Sister Anna Eklund was born in Finland and trained as a deaconess in Germany. She lived and worked in extremely difficult conditions, often using her own financial resources and possessions to support the church and the needs of others. She provided food, shoes and warm clothing for children; cared for the wounded and the sick; and trained and mentored other deaconesses. She also kept weekly worship going and dealt with the endless administration and bureaucracy required to maintain the building and the Methodist work. She effectively became the Superintendent of the Russian Methodist Episcopal mission work in 1918, when Dr George Simons, the male pastor with whom she had been working, left Russia and was not allowed to return.

S. T. Kimbrough Jr, in his introduction to the book he has written about Sister Anna, pays this tribute to her:

> Now and then, there are those whose lives as Christian servants need to be lifted up before the world community for the nature and quality of their service to God and others. Sister Anna may not have the notoriety of an Albert Schweitzer, a Mother Teresa or Gandhi, but she certainly ranks with them in terms of life lived wholly and fully for others, especially the poor. Had the political circumstances in Russia in the 1920s and 1930s allowed her ministry among the poor in and around St Petersburg, Russia to continue, perhaps today her life and name would have the resonance they deserve as a model of Christian service and servanthood.[*]

There are many other Russian Methodists—past and present—whose brave and humble leadership inspires and encourages me. I take my hat off to them or, as the Russians would say: *Nizkiy poklon* (make them a low bow).

---

[*]   S. T. Kimborough, *Sister Anna Eklund 1867–1949 A Methodist Saint in Russia* (New York: GBGM, 2001), p. 7; © S T Kimbrough. Used by permission.

9

The Women Myrrh-Bearers

April 2007

*The Tuesday night Russian Orthodox Bible study group
closes with prayer, and then people queue up to be blessed
and kissed on the forehead by the priest. For reasons I
cannot yet fully articulate (even to myself), I try to avoid
this ceremony and head straight out into the hallway to
put my coat on. Father Pavel, however, usually manages
to catch me before I leave and gently reminds me that I
am always welcome to get in touch if I have any questions
or would like to borrow any books. At the beginning
of Lent, he came up to me and told me that he had a
favour to ask of me. "I would like you to teach me how
to read the Easter Gospel," he said. I did not immediately
understand what he meant. Was he asking to hear my
reading of what John 20 means for the role of women
in the church? It turned out that it is traditional at the
Orthodox Easter Liturgy for the Gospel (which is not
John 20 but the Prologue to John's Gospel) to be read
in as many different languages as possible, and Father
Pavel wanted me to teach him how to read it in English.*

I readily agreed and, after several attempts at trying to explain to him the difference in pronunciation between true and through, he was ready for the big day.

I was obviously keen to be present for the Gospel reading and asked Father Pavel what time the service would be starting. He explained that it would start at midnight, with the candlelight procession at 1 a.m., and then the rest of the Easter Liturgy—including the Gospel. I got there about 12.30. There were lots of people milling around outside the church, but I managed to push my way inside to buy a candle and it was not long before the procession began. First came the children's choir, then the adult choir and then the icons and Gospel, the deacon and the priest. Everyone followed them in a complete circle around the church and then, after a few moments of waiting on the tiptoe of expectation the joyful proclamation was made—"Christ is Risen!" The Easter Hymn rang out and everyone went back into the church where we were to remain for the next three and a half hours.

I first experienced the Russian Orthodox Easter Liturgy in Paris when I was a sixth-former. It had a profound effect on me then, and I found myself reliving many of those feelings—and more—as I stood in the Church of the Women Myrrh-Bearers here in Pskov. There was an overwhelming sense of heaven on earth and of time touching eternity. I was surprised when I looked at my watch as the Gospel procession began, to discover that it was already 3 a.m.! I was so caught up in the beauty of it all that I did not tire of standing and had no desire to go home to bed. The deacon intoned the Gospel in Russian, and Father Pavel echoed him in Greek, English and German. "And the light shineth in darkness and the darkness comprehended it not." It was a deeply moving moment.

Father Pavel was the priest at the Russian Orthodox Church of the Women Myrrh-Bearers on Communal Street in Pskov. In 1969, he was sent to a labour camp for three years, because he had built an Orthodox Church. Whilst he was there, a truck ran over him, almost certainly deliberately, and his leg had to be amputated. He served in Pskov—with an artificial leg—from 1976 until 2013, when he was stabbed to death by a young man who was a guest in his home. His obituary, written by Michael Bordeaux, was published in the *Guardian* newspaper on 13 August 2013. Father Pavel was not afraid to criticize the Russian Orthodox hierarchy, and the respect with which he was held by many people both within and beyond Pskov stood in stark contrast to the strained relationship between him and his own bishop.*

Here is an excerpt from another of my newsletters (May 2008):

We were still in the middle of Lent when I went to the Saturday morning liturgy at the Russian Orthodox Church of the Women Myrrh-Bearers. Father Pavel was

---

*   *The Guardian*, 13 August 2013.

not presiding. He had told me in a telephone conversation a few weeks earlier that the bishop had removed him as priest-in-charge. Now a much younger man stood before the altar, dressed in the elaborate robes which are so much a part of Russian Orthodox worship. The church was packed with people, but after a few minutes, I became aware from my place at the back that a bearded figure in plain black robes was pushing his way through the crowd towards the door where I was standing. It was Father Pavel. His face was full of sorrow and immediately brought to mind Isaiah 53:3: "He was despised and rejected by others, a man of suffering and acquainted with infirmity." When Father Pavel drew nearer, he caught sight of me and suddenly smiled. As he passed by, he silently kissed me on the cheek. Now it was words from Dostoevsky's The Brothers Karamazov *which echoed in my heart. Towards the end of the legend of the Grand Inquisitor, Christ—who has given no verbal response to the Inquisitor's repeated question "Is it you?"—suddenly and quietly draws near to the old man and silently kisses him. This kiss burns in the old man's heart.*

I always felt myself to be in the presence of great holiness when I was with Father Pavel. I had nothing to teach him about the Easter Gospel. He taught me how to proclaim the resurrection. No language was needed. I could read it in his eyes and in his life. Sadly, I was not able to be at his funeral, because I was no longer living in Pskov at that time and getting a visa within three days is impossible. A photo I saw of the service reminded me of this icon of the women myrrh-bearers. Father Pavel's open coffin stood in the middle of the church and the congregation gathered around it to declare their Easter faith.

It was this icon of the women myrrh-bearers which particularly drew me to this festival row in the Pskov Museum. That was partly because of my connection with Father Pavel and the church where he served in Pskov. It was also because my first experience of open coffins was in Russia, and I found it extraordinarily powerful. I initially thought the women in the icon were looking at Jesus' body as they laid him in the tomb after the crucifixion. I then realized—as I took on board the angel at the head of the coffin and Jesus himself, already on the move above the women—that this is a depiction of Easter morning. What I thought was the body is in fact the discarded grave clothes. Nevertheless, the icon reminded me of the funerals I had attended in Pskov.

I will never forget the first Russian Orthodox funeral I attended. The husband of one of our church members had died. He was a pilot in the Russian Air Force, and therefore the funeral took place at the Alexander Nevsky Orthodox Church. Alexander Nevsky defended Pskov against a thirteenth-century German invasion, and a church was built in his name to serve the spiritual needs of the military population of the city. Another reason for this choice of church was that the older members of our congregation were somewhat dubious that Methodists would be allowed into heaven and tended to want an Orthodox funeral.

When we arrived for the service, I noticed five coffin lids with numbers on standing in the church porch. I thought the funeral directors were taking the opportunity to do a bit of business and that the numbers were the prices. However, when we went through into the church itself, I suddenly found myself face to face with five open coffins. Each of the deceased had a number stuck to their forehead corresponding to the numbers on the lids in the porch. The priest proceeded to "sing out" (a literal translation of the Russian word for a funeral) five people at once. The only point at which it got personal was when he dug out of his pocket a scrappy bit of paper and read out their names. Part of me was appalled by the lack of pastoral care being offered to these five families who stood clustered around the coffin of their loved one, their ashen faces starkly illuminated by the candles they held in their hands. At the same time, another part of me was deeply moved by the powerful sense that we do not journey home alone and that these people were all entering the gates of paradise together.

Icons of the women myrrh-bearers were the earliest depiction of the resurrection and were later displaced by icons of the descent into hell which is the focus of the next chapter. The account of Mary Magdalene's encounter with the risen Christ on Easter morning is one of my favourite Gospel passages (John 20:1–18). In this icon, however, there is a whole cluster of women—more than are named in the resurrection accounts of all four Gospels. Matthew records that Mary Magdalene and the other Mary went to the tomb. Mark says that it was Mary Magdalene, Mary the mother of James, and Salome. Luke names Mary Magdalene, Joanna and Mary the mother of James, but says that the other women who had come with Jesus from Galilee were there too. In John's Gospel, Mary Magdalene is on her own.

There are eight women who are traditionally given the title of women myrrh-bearers: Mary Magdalene, Mary the mother of Jesus, Joanna, Salome, Mary the wife of Cleopas, Susanna, Mary and Martha (the sisters of Lazarus). I am not sure why there are only six women in this icon or which two have been excluded. When I spoke about this icon at an online retreat during the COVID-19 pandemic, I suggested that perhaps the rule of six was in place! (One of the restrictions used by the British Government to limit social interaction—and therefore infection—was that people were only allowed to meet in groups of no more than six people.)

I love the fact that there is an official collective noun for these women—the myrrh-bearers. It makes me think about what women (and men) bear, carry and hold—both personally and collectively—as we gather in the place where we expect to find the body of Christ. Three of the women in the icon do seem to be holding a box or container, and they remind me of the Magi who brought gifts to Jesus after his birth—including, of course, the gift of myrrh.

The myrrh-bearing implies that these were women of means who could afford precious ointments and were willing to sacrifice what they had to care for the body of Christ. This is what they came to the tomb to do, and they are seen as role models today for those who care for the body of Christ which is the Church. Here is a quote from a sermon preached at an Orthodox church in England on the Sunday of the Myrrh-Bearers:

> Myrrh-bearing—selfless caring for the Body of Christ—is not only participating in the sacraments, preaching the Gospel and confessing the Faith, it is also doing that myriad of things which are so difficult because they require our sacrifice. For:

> Those who sing in church are myrrh-bearers.
> Those who clean the church are myrrh-bearers.
> Those who prepare the flowers for the
>   services are myrrh-bearers.
> Those who look after the garden are myrrh-bearers.
> Those who sew vestments and altar-
>   coverings are myrrh-bearers.
> Those who bake prosphora (communion
>   bread) are myrrh-bearers.
> Those who prepare tea or donate food
>   or wash up are myrrh-bearers.
> Those who donate icons or make offerings
>   of money are myrrh-bearers.

Even those who simply come and pray for
the salvation of all are myrrh-bearers.*

I thought this was a rather patronizing view of the roles
which women are given (or expected to fulfil) in the
Orthodox Church. However, when I shared this with
a group of women Methodist ministers, some of them
were quick to point out that there is no implication here
that all of this is being done by women. Men may also be
involved. They were also impressed by the recognition
that what might be seen as mundane tasks are deeply
holy and significant. Often, we see holiness as something
extraordinary and unattainable. Father Pavel—and all
those who are myrrh-bearers—teach me that holiness
can be seen and practised in our ordinary, everyday
lives.

---

*   Father Andrew Phillips. Used with permission.

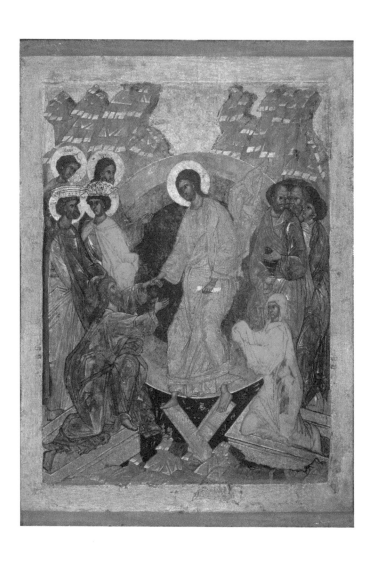

To hell and back

September 2003

This is my own translation of a description of the Moscow metro from a short story called This is the best of worlds *by the contemporary Russian author Victoria Tokareva. I read it on my first night back in Russia and found it very evocative of the world I had re-entered:*

One day he waited as everything slipped away before his eyes, and Candide saw clearly an unfamiliar city and a big letter "M" and a lot of people who were walking inside under this letter. Candide went in with them all and found himself going down an escalator. Candide assumed that he had died and was being carried down into the underworld . . . But Candide still loved life and, finding himself on the escalator, was frightened and started running back up. The escalator was going down, and it seemed that Candide was running up and down on the spot. Nobody paid any attention to him.

People strictly and calmly looked straight ahead . . . "Stop!" shouted Candide. "Do you really have no regrets about leaving the best of all worlds?" Nobody understood because Candide was shouting in an incomprehensible language . . . The escalator carried people down to a firm open space. Something long and rumbling, like an iron snake, rushed out of the darkness and people darted inside into large, light cages. Candide got in along with everyone else. People calmly sat down on both sides and began to read large rustling pages. The train went through a tunnel, at the end of which must be light. Everyone would have to stand before the Creator, and he would begin to sort them out—who to hell, and who to heaven. But the people, it seemed, weren't expecting anything of the sort. They all sat, immersed in their pages. "Come to your senses!" shouted Candide. "Are you prepared to meet God?" People raised their heads and looked at the yelling lad but didn't say anything. Only one old lady nodded her head. "This is all Gorbachev's fault. He ruined Russia," she shouted. She delved into her bag, reached an apple and offered it to Candide.

The metro in St Petersburg is one of the deepest in the world. It can take four minutes to descend on the escalator—and another four minutes to ascend again.

That adds a significant time to every journey. As someone who loves cities and travel, riding the metro is more of a heavenly than a hellish experience for me. However, as indicated in the Holy Week reflection earlier in the book, it is also a place where pickpocketing is rife. So I always felt nervous when descending into this underworld with visiting friends whose safety I felt responsible for. "Don't talk, and look like you know where you're going," I would tell them as we entered the station. "We're getting off at the ... th stop." Unfortunately, I was unable to prevent one friend from being mugged on the St Petersburg metro, and there was another scary occasion when one of my visitors managed to get on the overcrowded Moscow metro whilst her husband and I were left on the platform. Thankfully, we found her again.

In the icon, Jesus looks as if he has just emerged from an underground tunnel and is trying to pull Adam into or out of the train. As I mentioned in the last chapter, this icon of the descent into hell is now the most common Easter icon. Easter begins with the tradition of Christ descending into hell and lifting Adam and Eve back into the paradise from which they had fallen.

The Russian Orthodox Easter liturgy, which begins on Saturday evening, usually includes this wonderful homily from St John Chrysostom:

> If you are devout and love God, enjoy this beautiful and radiant festival. If you are a loyal

servant, enter rejoicing into the joy of the Lord. If you are weary with fasting, take your reward. If you worked from the first hour, receive today what is rightly owing to you. If you came after the third hour, celebrate the feast with thanksgiving. If you only appeared after the sixth hour, don't be troubled by doubt. For nothing is lost. If you delayed until the ninth hour, come without any wavering. If you appeared only at the eleventh hour, don't be worried about your slowness. Our Lord is generous and welcomes the last just as he does the first. He gives rest to those who have worked from the eleventh hour just as to those who have worked from the first. He has compassion for the last and he cares for the first. He is generous to the former and he shows favour to the latter. He accepts the work done and welcomes the sense of purpose. He honours the action and praises the intention. So, come all of you into the joy of our Lord—those who are first and those who are second—and receive your reward. Rich and poor, dance for joy with each other. Whether you are self-controlled or more relaxed honour the day. Whether you are fasting or not fasting rejoice today. The table is full, so everybody take great pleasure in it. There is an abundance of good meat—no one is to go away hungry. All of you are to enjoy this wealth of goodness. No one is to lament their poverty, for the kingdom belonging to everybody has appeared. No one is to bewail their shortcomings, for mercy rose up from the tomb. No one is to fear death, for the death of the Saviour set us free. He brought death to an end while he was in its clutches. He brought Hades under discipline when he descended to Hades. He made Hades bitter when it tasted his flesh. Isaiah prophesied this when he cried: "Hades was made bitter". It was made bitter when it met you in the depths; for it was rendered impotent. It was made bitter; for it was mocked. It was made bitter; for it was put to death. It was made bitter; for it was overpowered. It was made bitter; for it was bound in chains. It took a body, but actually found it to be God. It took earth and met heaven. It took what it saw and has fallen as a result of what it failed to see. "Where, death, is your sting? Where, Hades, is your victory?" Christ is risen and demons have fallen. Christ is risen and the angels rejoice. Christ is risen and life can be lived. Christ is risen and no one who is dead is in the tomb. For Christ raised from the dead became the first-fruits of those who had fallen asleep. To him be glory and power for ever and ever. Amen.[*]

---

[*] Kindly translated by the Revd Andrew Maguire of <https://early churchtexts.com>. Used with permission.

I love the inclusiveness being preached here. There is none of the pain of being too late which we met in *Eugene Onegin*. That is also one of the messages I get from this icon. No one is forgotten or left behind. Christ empties hell and fills heaven.

One of the tendencies which mission partners—and all of us—need to be aware of is thinking that it is our job to save people from the hell we think they are in when, for them, it might not be hell at all. We can assume—particularly when we are experiencing culture shock—that the way people are living is wrong and that we need to rescue them, to enable them to live like we do. Differing attitudes to Muslim women wearing hijab is a good example of this. We might see this as an oppressive practice, but for many Muslim women it is a liberating choice. More specifically Russian examples include praying with icons, eating cabbage pie and beating your church members in the *banya* on a Saturday afternoon! All of these may seem a long way from your idea of heaven but, for me, they have all become experiences which I would readily describe by using the Russian slang word *kayf*. This can be translated as bliss, paradise or the high state of ecstasy which can be produced by taking drugs.

There were, however, aspects of Russian life which troubled and shocked my Russian friends as much as they did me. There were three areas of work where the Methodist Church in Pskov (and many other Methodist churches in Russia) stretched out a hand—pastorally, practically and prayerfully—to enable people to rise above the hellish situation they were in. These three areas of work were with alcoholics and their families, old people and orphanages.

A PowerPoint slide in a presentation I gave about mission in Russia in 2006 included these statistics:

- One in three Russian men and one in seven Russian women are alcoholics.
- Nearly half of all deaths of working-age men are caused by alcohol poisoning.
- The male life expectancy is fifty-eight.
- A bottle of beer is cheaper than a bottle of Coca-Cola.

A significant proportion of our congregation had an alcoholic in the family, and it was in Pskov that I first became familiar with the remarkable work of Alcoholics Anonymous and Al-Anon.

An excerpt from my February 2004 newsletter describes a visit I made with some church members to an old people's home:

> As many beds as possible were squeezed into every room and all along the corridor. You literally had to walk a plank to get to the one toilet for forty people. The whole place seemed more like a third-class train compartment than a "home". I found a stool to perch on and sat and

talked with the babushki. *"You must find yourself*
a Russian husband," they said, "but make sure he
doesn't drink." By the end of the visit Galya was in
tears. "If I don't get married and have children,"
she sobbed, "I could end up in a place like this."

The orphanages made me want to pick up the children
and bring them home with me. Here is an excerpt from
my December 2006 newsletter:

It was delivery day at the orphanage. Every three
weeks a new group of children aged from six
months to four years arrive at their new home.
On the day we visited, there were already 124
children in residence. Many of them had been
born to alcoholic mothers and were severely
physically disabled. All of them clearly lacked
mental and emotional stimulation. The staff
work twelve-hour shifts and are each individually
responsible for up to fifteen children. This makes
it impossible for them to do much more than keep
each child fed and clean. We spent some time on
this initial visit engaging with the children and
staff and plan to return with the youth group
at Christmas. We saw the room where adopting
parents (mainly from America) meet with their
future child. Nelli was convinced she had found
mine, when the little boy she was with turned to

stare at me as I walked past to give some attention
to three more babies on the other side of the room.

I spent time with several American couples who came to adopt children from Pskov. I vividly remember how emotional I felt when I waved goodbye to a five-year-old boy as he set off with his new parents on the overnight train to Moscow, en route to a new life in Florida. I wondered if he would retain any memory of the Russian language or of the city where he was born, both of which I had grown to love so much. I hoped that one day he would be able to come back. Fifteen years later, I was intrigued to find an email in my inbox from *pskovman*. It turned out to be from this boy—now a young man and wanting to find out more about where he had come from.

I gave serious consideration to adopting a Russian child myself, but—as well as a multitude of other reasons for deciding against it—I knew that I would find it incredibly difficult to "save" one child and leave all the others behind. I believe that Jesus rescues everyone from hell. I am not capable of doing that. What I can do is to make pastoral visits to hellish places and spend time with the people who are there. That is what this icon—and the ministry of the Methodist Church in Russia—has taught me.

1 1

Lost in translation

June 2004

Verbs of motion occupy a significant proportion of any Russian grammar book. There are even whole books dedicated to the subject. I know that all my former language teachers would love me to write this newsletter in Russian, because it is going to include a lot of verbs of motion and they would be able to see whether I was using them properly. The correct verb will indicate whether the journey was on foot or by transport, whether it was in one direction or in more than one direction, and whether you are still at your destination or back at the starting point. When you have decided all that, you can then choose from a whole range of prefixes to describe the said motion even more precisely.

I have now moved to my new apartment. (I travelled by transport in one direction with a prefix meaning "over" or "across".) Galya's father and brother very kindly made several trips in the car with all my boxes and suitcases. The lift doors close after seven seconds which does not give much time to load things in and out. However, everything is now here—except Galya (my flatmate). She is very pressured at work at the moment with the end of the school year but is determined to join me as soon as possible.

I did not actually spend much time here myself last month. I slept here for three nights, and then spent the next two nights on the train. Nelli and I went to Moscow. (We travelled by train in more than one direction and are now back where we started from.) The main purpose of our trip was to pick up a man! Bob had flown over from Memphis, Tennessee and was carrying on his person, in cash, a generous donation from his church towards the construction of our new church building. We were wandering around Moscow all day with this money, and it was a huge relief to be able to hand it over to our church treasurer the following morning. We also brought back a lot of books and resources from a Christian bookstore in Moscow. I was very excited to find Rowan Williams' Christian Theology *and Henri Nouwen's* The Return of the Prodigal Son *in Russian translation.*

"To translate" or "to interpret" is actually another verb of motion. The Russian word literally means "to transfer". I spent the next week interpreting for Bob, and he was extremely helpful to me too. There wasn't much time to write a sermon that week what with moving house and going to Moscow. I wanted to talk about Ascension Day, and Bob used to be an airline pilot. So, I interviewed him during the sermon slot about his "ascension" experiences—another verb of motion!

Hans Växby was elected to serve as Bishop of the Eurasia Episcopal Area in February 2005, having previously served as Bishop of the Nordic and Baltic area. Hans is Swedish and is married to a Finnish Methodist pastor called Kaikka. Kaikka was still serving a church in Helsinki when Hans took up his appointment in Moscow. They both became frequent travellers on the train which ran between the two cities, and their time together was precious. Hans was not a Russian speaker and so needed an interpreter to work with him. I was part of a small team who shared this responsibility at the annual conferences for North-West Russia and Belarus. The first time I did this, Kaikka was also present, and Hans asked me to sit between them, so that they could both hear my translation. I told him that I was reluctant to separate them when they were already having to spend so much time apart. Hans replied: "You are not separating us. You are uniting us."

The pain of separation is something I feel deeply. I find it excruciatingly difficult to let go and say goodbye. When I look at the icon of the ascension, I feel that pain. These companions of Jesus who have been through the emotional rollercoaster of Good Friday and Easter Day now have to watch Jesus leave them again. However, Hans' words to me could also be said to Jesus at the ascension: "You are not separating us. You are uniting us." The ascension means that Jesus is no longer restricted to being in one place at one time. The presence of Christ can now be known in every place at any time.

I want to share another story about Hans. On one occasion, he was flying back to Moscow from Samara (a city in south-west Russia), having fitted the wedding of two pastors into an already busy schedule. He was so tired that he fell asleep as soon as he was settled into his seat on the plane. A few hours later, he woke up, and everyone was disembarking. He went with them into the terminal building but could not understand why no one was being allowed to collect their luggage and proceed to the exit. In his limited Russian, he kept saying: "*Bagazh, Bagazh*" (luggage, luggage) and got the repeated response: "*Net, Net*" (No, No). Eventually, he phoned his assistant in the bishop's office who spoke to one of the other passengers and discovered that Hans was still in Samara! Due to a technical fault, the plane had sat on the tarmac for several hours without going anywhere.

This reminded me of the 1975 film *Ironiya Sudby* (The Irony of Fate) which is always shown on Russian television on 31 December. It tells the story of a man who gets drunk with his friends in the *banya* on New Year's Eve and is mistakenly put on a plane to Leningrad. He believes that he is in Moscow and gets a taxi to his home. His key opens the apartment, and the address, layout, decor and furniture are all exactly the same as his Moscow home. The real owner of the apartment then appears, and great comedy ensues—all based on the identikit design of Soviet housing in the Brezhnev era.

I am not suggesting that when Jesus arrived in heaven, he thought that he was still on earth. But I think that the icon of the ascension, indeed all icons, can enable us to experience heaven whilst we are still on earth. Our prayer and worship can take us—translate us—to another place where we are no longer separated from those on another shore but united with them. Worship is a place where two rivers meet.

Most of the translation I did in Russia was simultaneous. In other words, I was talking at the same time as the speaker—a few beats behind. When this was taking place during a worship service, I often declined to translate the prayers. This was partly to give me a break from the intense concentration required but was also because I felt that my constant muttering was a distraction to other worshippers. Those I was interpreting for were often grateful when I stopped talking too. They told me that they felt able to participate in the worship even without knowing what all the words meant. There is so much about worship which goes beyond words. The music and the symbolism can express far more than the most gifted verbal communicator. This is because worship, at its best, takes us to another place. It gives us that encounter with "the other" which I wrote about in Chapter 1.

Having said that, the language we use in church can be unintelligible to the outsider. One of the reasons I needed to have some supplementary Russian lessons in Moscow before taking up my appointment in Pskov was because much of the vocabulary I needed to use when preaching and leading worship had not been covered in the syllabus at school and university. That learning confirmed for me how important it is, even in a context where everyone is a native speaker, to explain some of the words and terms we use in church. For many people, they can feel like a foreign language. Our worship needs to find a balance between giving people an experience of that mystery which we now only see as "in a mirror, dimly" and expressing our faith in ways which convey more meaning than the sound of "a noisy gong or a clanging cymbal" (1 Corinthians 13:12,1).

The Russian word for sacrament is *tainstvo* which literally means "mystery". The Russian Methodist Worship Book contains liturgies for the Mystery of Holy Communion and the Mystery of Baptism— both prefaced by explanations of the significance and meaning of these sacraments. Mystery and meaning are both important and could perhaps be seen as the opposing banks though which the river of worship is held and channelled.

Worship is a theme which flows though the Gospel of St Luke which both begins and ends in the temple. Luke's Gospel and his second volume, the Acts of the Apostles, are two rivers which meet at the ascension. The sequel finds its source at the point where the first book ended. Chapter 1 of Acts begins with the disciples staring into heaven trying to make sense of this mysterious event (Acts 1:10). In Chapter 2, there is another mysterious event as the Holy Spirit descends in wind and fire (Acts 2:2–3). This mystery is accompanied by meaning as the disciples find themselves able to speak in other languages and the multilingual Jerusalem crowd is amazed that each of them can hear about God's deeds of power in their own tongue. They are no longer lost in translation. The meaning is clear. They are no longer separated. They are united. Mystery and meaning meet.

I sometimes left people rather mystified by what I was trying to say in Russian. I once told someone she could travel to our church in a white washing bowl (*tazik*) with a green stripe when what I meant to say was *pazik*—the make of the vehicle. I sat at a kitchen table thinking I was extolling the virtues of Earl Grey tea (*chai s bergamotom*), but my host thought I enjoyed having tea with a hippopotamus (*begemot*) because I had not rolled the "r" in the middle of the word properly!

There is a wonderful phrase in Russian for describing someone who has taken a long time to get the joke or understand what someone else has said. *Doshlo kak do zhirafa* literally means "it got through as it does for a giraffe". The implication is that the giraffe takes time to turn mystery into meaning because there is a long journey up the neck to the brain! There were ten days between Ascension and Pentecost, and I am very conscious that there are some mysteries in our lives which require us to wait to find the meaning. I am always grateful for the forty days of Eastertide because that gives me time to make the journey from the loss of Good Friday to the new life of Easter Day. I cannot make that emotional transition in three days! I also do not want to imply that it is easy to find meaning in the mysteries we experience in life—or that we always do. I know that I will go to the grave with lots of unresolved questions. For me it is important that worship is a place where we can hold those questions as we stare into heaven, knowing that there is much which is beyond our grasp.

We sometimes describe worship as a foretaste of the heavenly banquet. Icons give us a glimpse through the window. I think our worship can also help us to echo what is going on in heaven as we join our voices in prayer and praise with God's people of every time and place.

Serving as an interpreter gave me a powerful sense of being an echo. One of my favourite memories is when I was on stage at a Russia Initiative Consultation (a gathering of Russian Methodists and representatives from their American partner churches) together with Andrei Kuznetsov. Andrei is the pastor of Bethany Church in Pushkin, a town on the outskirts of St Petersburg. He was preaching in Russian, and I was translating into English. On this occasion, we were doing this consecutively. In other words, Andrei would say a sentence or two and then pause for me to put it into English. All the participants were staying in the same hotel, and during the night the fire alarm had gone off; we all had to leave our rooms and gather in the car park. Andrei used this experience as an illustration in his sermon. He told us that he was in the bathroom, trying to work out what the multitude of buttons and switches he found in there did. He had just pressed what he hoped was the toilet flush when the fire alarm went off. He seriously thought that he had set the alarm off himself. At this point in the story, I and all the Russian speakers started chuckling and the Americans were left waiting for me to stop giggling and tell them what Andrei had said. Then there was a roar of American laughter too. That ripple effect felt like a wonderful Ascension to Pentecost movement as the rivers of mystery and meaning met, and everyone was able to share and echo the joy in their own language.

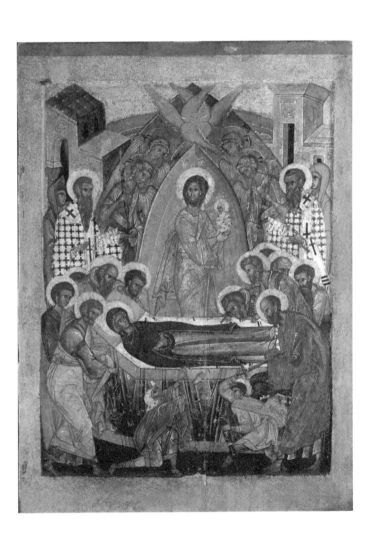

1 2

Homecoming

June 2009

I can normally predict when I am likely to cry, and I had known for several weeks that hearing the bishop read the list of appointments without my name on it would be one of those moments. When this was immediately followed by the music group singing one of my favourite Russian hymns, my silent tears turned into uncontrollable sobbing, and it took all my strength to find my voice again and continue interpreting for the overseas guests. "That was the wettest translation I have ever heard!" joked one of the Americans afterwards.

Annual Conference in St Petersburg this year included a special celebration of 120 years of Methodism in Russia and the ordination of five presbyters. There was also a farewell presentation to me (more tears), and I lived each day to the full, with an overflowing heart, returning one "White Night" (it was the time of year when it never gets completely dark) from a walk with a friend by the Gulf of Finland to find that the external door had been locked!

Last month, I lost the keys to our apartment and could only assume that I had thrown them down the rubbish chute or that they had fallen into a box, and I would find them when unpacking in East Ham. Exactly a week later, I discovered them in my apron pocket. However, those seven days without them, when I was busy packing up my freight, felt deeply symbolic. I had lost the keys to my Russian home.

Tomorrow I am conducting the marriage service for Yulia and Dima—the first ever wedding in our church. It has become the tradition in many Russian cities for newlyweds to engrave a padlock with their names, fasten it to the railings by the river and throw the key into the water. I feel similarly bound to Russia, and I am going to have to dive deep within myself to find the key which will enable me to open my heart again—without breaking it—to all that awaits me in England.

The lectionary, as ever, is a wonderful gift. As I preach and pray my way through these final days, I feel as overwhelmed by the enormity of the task before me as David must have felt when he stood before Goliath, and as moved as he was by the beauty of his relationship with Jonathan and the pain of saying goodbye.

I close with the words of the Russian romance which I sang at Annual Conference last weekend and which my balalaika teacher is going to play during my final service next Sunday. This translation is by Mr Dewey—my school Russian teacher:

We met—and all the past came flooding
Into my frozen heart once more,
Reviving it, as I remembered
Those years, that golden time of yore . . .

Just as late autumn may surprise us
With days of passing moments when
We feel a sudden breath of springtime
And something in us stirs again—

So, washed by the intense emotion
Of times past—quickening anew,
With long-forgotten fascination
Those features dear to me I view . . .

As in a dream I gaze upon you –
As if across the years' divide –
And now those sounds speak out more clearly
That in my heart had never died . . .

Not only memory is speaking:
Life too proclaims itself once more –
You have not lost that old enchantment,
And still I love you as before! . . . *

*   Translation © John Dewey. In Fyodor Tyutchev, *Selected Poems*,
translated, introduced and edited by John Dewey (Brimstone Press,
2014). Used with permission.

Sometimes, when I entered an Orthodox Church, I would see a gap in the iconostasis. One of the icons was missing. I discovered that icons could be removed from the iconostasis and placed on a stand at the front of the church to celebrate the saint or event.

This temporary removal from home to spend some time in another place connected with my experience of being a mission partner. I had been released for a certain period but eventually needed to go back and fill the gap which had been created by my absence—both at the family meal table and in the life of the British Methodist Church.

This final icon of the Dormition of Mary reminds me of Russian icons of the nativity where Mary, as here, reclines in the centre of the scene and a newborn child also draws our gaze. The icon of the nativity depicts the birth of Christ and the icon of the Dormition depicts the death of Mary. However, her death is also her birth into eternal life—as is indicated by Christ holding her newborn soul.

My departure from Russia felt like a death and not a birth. I was still sobbing as I boarded my flight to London in St Petersburg, and I needed far longer than the three-and-a-half-hour flight to make the transition. I later heard of another mission partner who had wisely decided to travel from China to Britain by train at the end of her period of overseas service because she did not feel able to move from departures to arrivals in a matter of hours. I was excited about the new life that awaited me in East London, but my homecoming also felt as if I was leaving home. I was no longer sure where I really belonged.

The story of the wise men from the east had been significant for me since attending that vocational conference in my first year at university. The feelings I had when I left Russia reminded me of T. S. Eliot's poem "Journey of the Magi". The poet suggests that the Magi were also unsure whether they were experiencing birth or death. Their homecoming left them feeling like aliens.

Whilst writing this book, I saw Ralph Fiennes perform T. S. Eliot's *Four Quartets* on stage at the Royal & Derngate Theatre in Northampton. I was struck by the multiple references to our end being our beginning, and I was also left pondering whether the *Four Quartets* relate to the four seasons of a year.

The festival row from the iconostasis takes us through the church year—a journey which we repeat over and over throughout our lives. When we come back to the beginning again, there is a familiarity about it. We have been here before—and yet we are also in a different place. All that has happened to us, around us, within us and without us affects the way in which we hear and see that part of the Christian year.

The wise men went home by a different road (Matthew 2:12). Ostensibly this was because they needed to avoid King Herod. However, I think this is also a way of telling us that they had been changed by their encounter with the Christ-child. Their return journey would not have been the same as their outward journey even if they had taken the same route.

I have been changed by the time I spent living in Russia, but that change does not mean that I have stopped being the person I was before. I am still Nicola Vidamour. Like a Russian *matrëshka* (nesting doll), the tiny child I was in the beginning is still and always will be part of me. The difference is that I now carry within me additional layers of insight and understanding.

I am also aware—particularly as I look at the icon of the Dormition—of the people I carry in my heart who have touched my life along the way. Almost everyone in the icon seems to be holding or supporting Mary in some way. Many of them have already appeared in other icons in this festival row. They remind me of the great cloud of witnesses (Hebrews 12:1) who are part of our story, whether we are conscious of them or not.

Homecoming, for me, always involves some unpacking of the treasures I have accumulated on my travels. Some of these will be physical souvenirs. Others will be the experiences and encounters which have now become part of my emotional baggage.

The festival row of the iconostasis—and the church year which these icons represent—help me to unpack these treasures one by one. They enable me to look through one window at a time and focus on the two rivers which meet there. They also ensure that, every year, I will make a journey from birth to death and come face to face with many of the other significant moments which come in between.

The festival row—and the church year—also require me to jump into a river which may be the very opposite of the one in which I am swimming at the time. I may, for example, feel that I have been plunged into the depths of hell in my personal or work life, but the icon for that day is the Feast of the Ascension. That does not mean I have to deny the way I am feeling. The descent into hell is part of the cycle too. It does mean that I always need to be aware that there is another river flowing towards me.

This invitation to meet the other is what first attracted me to God, to travel, to Russian, and to icons. Every place where two rivers meet is holy ground to me. I would even say that such places are where I experience homecoming. That may seem strange, as home is normally associated with the familiar rather than the other. However, homecoming for me is not necessarily about feeling comfortable. It is about recognizing that this is where God is calling me to be; this is where my life finds purpose and meaning; this is where my end and my beginning merge. This is where two rivers meet.

Postscript

The Russian words for Good-bye are *Do svidaniya* which literally mean "until meeting". The word translated as "meeting" can also mean a date between lovers. I have a deep love for Russia and have been longing for another date with her. The current situation is heart-breaking. I have friends both in Russia and Ukraine, and reading their messages and watching the news leaves me in pieces.

One of the friends I made when studying Russian at Bristol University now serves on the chaplaincy team at a secure hospital. Some of the pastoral visits she makes involve sitting at a distance and communicating with the patient though a small open shutter in a heavy locked door. She can only see the face of the patient and told me that the framing of the face by the shutter makes her feel that she is looking at an icon. When her visit ends, the shutter is closed, and the patient disappears from view.

I am very fearful that the iron curtain is about to close again, putting an end to the glimpses we currently have of life in Russia and the conversations which maintain our relationships with one another. I hope that this book will help to keep some of those windows open and remind us that: "For now we see in a mirror, dimly, but then we will see face to face. Now I know only in part; then I will know fully, even as I have been fully known." (1 Corinthians 13:12) Death and separation cannot keep the door of love closed. As the Russian proverb says: *Dal'she s glaz, blizhe k serdtsu.* What is further from the eye is nearer to the heart.

Nicola Vidamour
Good Friday 2022

Lightning Source UK Ltd.
Milton Keynes UK
UKHW021725011222
413137UK00012B/314